Filipe Menezes Soares

What does dictatorship have to do with democracy?

Filipe Menezes Soares

What does dictatorship have to do with democracy?

The arts of governing in Brazil in the 1970s

ScienciaScripts

Imprint

Any brand names and product names mentioned in this book are subject to trademark, brand or patent protection and are trademarks or registered trademarks of their respective holders. The use of brand names, product names, common names, trade names, product descriptions etc. even without a particular marking in this work is in no way to be construed to mean that such names may be regarded as unrestricted in respect of trademark and brand protection legislation and could thus be used by anyone.

Cover image: www.ingimage.com

This book is a translation from the original published under ISBN 978-613-9-69021-3.

Publisher:
Sciencia Scripts
is a trademark of
Dodo Books Indian Ocean Ltd. and OmniScriptum S.R.L publishing group

120 High Road, East Finchley, London, N2 9ED, United Kingdom
Str. Armeneasca 28/1, office 1, Chisinau MD-2012, Republic of Moldova, Europe
Printed at: see last page
ISBN: 978-620-7-75772-5

INDICE

1 INTRODUCTION

Before we begin the discussion that this brief book proposes, I believe it is essential to enter a field that cuts across the approach to the sources dealt with here. I am referring to studies of authorship, more specifically of the authorial role played by General Garrastazu Medici in the books that contain his pronouncements as president. With these sources and through a study that focuses on the historical and cultural role played by the author, in this book I propose an analysis of texts signed by Emilio Garrastazu Medici between 1969 and 1974. To problematize the general-president's authorship and point out some characteristics of the way in which the discourses of the civil-military government existed, circulated, functioned and were appropriated. At the same time, a study of authorship also makes it possible to describe the historical moment in which the president was inserted, understanding the particularities of the period in which he was in charge of the government (1969 - 1974). The narrative aims to establish two movements. The first is to broaden Medici's discourse, making room for the various subjects, social groups, institutions and representations that make up this speech to be recognized. The other movement is to understand how the figure of Medici was constructed in these discourses, where we can locate the subjectivity of the author in the published texts and what role this subject plays in authorship. From this double movement I intend to expose how authorship contributes to the government policies of the dictatorship: Emilio Garrastazu Medici is an author invented by the military government.

Medici is an author[5] . During the civil-military dictatorship, he was also president of Brazil between 1969 and 1974. But what allows me to say that Garrastazu Medici is an author? Under what conditions and in what forms can that president appear as an author in Brazil in the early 1970s? These are some of the questions I intend to debate in this session. They are also important questions for the approach to authorship in History.

---

[5] In all, the National Press Department published nine books authored by President Medici. The works cited here are indicated in the bibliography.

In general, the author is constituted in history. When I expand on the authorship of Medici's speeches, I establish a meeting point between a series of events linked to the civil-military dictatorship. Problematizing Medici's authorship implies describing the historical moment in which the president was inserted, taking up the particularities of the period in which he was in charge of the government (1969 - 1974). Understanding the conditions that made it possible for Medici to be the author of a particular work is also an effort to expose the workings of the military government's discursive practices between 1969 and 1974.

The simplified way in which I set out my intentions in discussing the president's authorship does not exclude the complexity of the problem addressed. The relationship between the text and the author involves a series of particularities. Each text points to the figure of the author in its own way. In common sense, the condition of authorship means attributing to the subject-author a position that is external and prior to the text. This is apparently how we understand an author. However, to denaturalize this relationship is to conceive of authorship as part of the functioning of discursive practices. Authorship responds as a principle that dominates writing as a practice, in other words, the author is a rule of writing. But this author cannot be understood as a single subject who is responsible for the text. He is a flow that, in writing, allows a space to open up where the subject keeps disappearing. In turn, the disappearance of the subject is a resource that facilitates the understanding of discursive practices. The way in which discourses are articulated in social relations can be better discerned when investigated through the use of the "author-function"[6] . Through Medici's authorship, it is possible to point out some characteristics of the way in which the discourses of the civil-military government existed and circulated during the early 1970s.

In order to study authorship, I selected some texts published in book form by the National Press Department. The books bring together speeches that were delivered

---

6 FOUCAULT, MICHEL. **What is an author?** In Ditos e escritos vol. III Estetica: Literatura e Pintura, Musica e Cinema. Rio de Janeiro: Editora Forense Universitaria, 2001. In this text, the author discusses the political and cultural role played by authorship throughout its history. Michel Foucault's investigation, through what he used to call genealogy, searches for the emergence of authorship as a rule of writing and its implications for discourses and social practices.

both at specific public events and those that were circulated nationwide. These speeches were all signed by the president and then published and distributed throughout the country. It is these pronouncements that I present for analysis in this article. It is these publications that give the then head of state the status of author.

I have chosen to use the books in a way that opens up space for us to think of the sources as paths that do not close off questions, but rather establish problems. Based on a certain conception of government, the speeches gathered in the publications cover the most varied themes of national reality. They are strictly linked to the set of public policies put into practice by the dictatorship government. In addition to the speeches, before they were finally published and distributed, it is important to say that they underwent a thorough selection and grouping process. Each title brings together a set of related speeches. It is hard to believe that the president had total autonomy in the editing and publishing process, or that he was even solely responsible for writing the texts. Elio Gaspari goes so far as to say that Medici "presided over the country in silence, reading speeches written by others, at social gatherings, implacable with gossip"[7] .

Whether they were written by Medici or by government advisors doesn't matter. What is relevant to the discussion I am presenting here is the fact that the authorship was attributed to him. The president-author is a relationship that allows us to discuss how the dictatorship's discourses and public policies circulate and function. Authorship is a rule that takes us back to the early 1970s and authorizes the historical problematization of the period.

1.1 The dictatorship and the president-author

It would be a mistake to isolate the figure of President Garrastazu Medici without establishing a discussion of the dictatorship and the circumstances that marked the period.

On 13 December 1968, Institutional Act Number Five was enacted, dissolving

---

7 GASPARI, Helio. **A ditadura Escancarada vol. 2 - As ilusoes Armadas.** Sao Paulo: Companhia das Letras, 2012.

Congress and establishing the legal mechanisms to institutionalize, even more effectively, police and military repression of citizens, institutions and movements resisting the regime. The third government of the revolution inherited AI-5 less than a year after its promulgation. Political mobilization was growing against the dictatorship government, which in turn was already responding with arrests, torture and assassinations[8] . From AI-5 until the end of the Medici government, the period was known as the "years of lead". There is no doubt that after AI-5, armed repression and, in general, censorship, reached a level of authoritarianism without limits. However, the definition "years of lead" summed up this period in terms of the practices of repression. In my opinion, this "reductionism" does not take into account the complexity of the dictatorship in the country. The government of the dictatorship, and in particular the Medici government itself, always made an effort to get closer to the population and establish its legitimacy. It wasn't only with weapons that the dictatorship was maintained, but the construction of its legitimacy was decisive for the maintenance of a government that lasted approximately twenty years. Authorship, therefore, refers to one of the strategies for approaching the population and building the government's legitimacy.

Most dictatorial governments have always used a political strategy that sought to strengthen the personal identity of their top representatives. General Garrastazu Medici took over the presidency after a period in which the government was led by a military junta. The government needed a major public figure to represent it. Medici was chosen, among other things, to represent this public figure. Given this scenario, I suggest that authorship was one of the strategies that also helped build the president's personal identity, strengthening the population's appropriation of government speeches.

Medici was not only the government's spokesman and the person responsible for dialoguing with the population, but the author himself. Authorship created a direct channel between the government and the population. It was one of the strategies

---

8   On the torture practices of the military regime, see MONTEGRO, ANTONIO. **Historia e Memoria de Lutas Polfticas in Marcas da Memoria: Historia Oral da Amistia no Brasil.** Recife: Ed. Universitaria da UFPE, 2012.

aimed at guaranteeing security and support for the government. In turn, security and support were built through policies and speeches that were accompanied by a series of repressive measures that dismantled the political organizations of resistance.[5.]

In the third government of the dictatorship, a triumphalist rhetoric was produced that consecrated the country's moment of economic development. The speeches produced a broad effect of truth and earned the government high approval ratings. According to Maria Jose de Rezende, approval ratings reached 80%[910] . The success achieved by the government was directly associated with propaganda and the multiplication of official pronouncements. These pronouncements were associated with the figure of the president. Referring to Medici as the author of the speeches was to place the president at the origin of what was said by the government. In order to create an environment in which the will of the people and the policies of the government could be brought closer together, the "author function" played an extremely important role. Through the speeches, the population became aware of the government's policies. Medici's speeches represented the conceptions of the civil-military dictatorship at the beginning of the 1970s. As the author, he himself was responsible for what was being said and he was the one the population had to trust.

Another point, also linked to what I understand by authorship, allows for a new parallel with the civil-military regime in Brazil. In the text *"What is an author?"[11]* we find an intellectual effort that opts to construct a genealogy of authorship. The need to assign an author to literary works arises, initially, from the form of ownership and what we might call criminal appropriation. The author is born into the property system at the same time as writing comes under scrutiny for the possibility of carrying transgressive content. Historically, just like discourses, writing carries with it a bipolar field: the licit and the illicit; the sacred and the profane; the forbidden and the legitimate. When the rules on author's rights were established, thus recognizing

---

9   At the beginning of the Medici government, the DOI-CODI (The Detachment of Information Operations - Center for Internal Defense Operations) was created, an organ subordinate to the Army, of intelligence and repression of the Brazilian government during the dictatorship regime.

10 REZENDE, MARIA JOSE DE. **The military dictatorship in Brazil: repression and the pretense of legitimacy 1964 - 1984.** Londrina: UEL, 2001.

11 FOUCAULT, 2001.

authorship, it was easier to control the possibility of transgression that belonged to writing. It is precisely this transgressive side that interests me here. The "author function" is linked to the legal and institutional system. Jurisdiction contains, determines and articulates the universe of discourses.

Therefore, since discourses are also a practice, in other words, they are acts, it is necessary to know who is responsible for them. Responsibility for a text, a painting, a painting, in short, for a discourse, is attributed on the basis of authorship. There is therefore a link between the function of author and the right to monitor, censor, judge and punish, exercised by an authority or power. Now, in addition to propaganda, another pillar of the dictatorship was precisely its ability and insistence on surveillance and censorship[12] . Through this game, the civilian-military government constantly instituted what I called the bipolarity of speeches. The president's pronouncements carried definitions of what was lawful and what was unlawful, what could be practiced and what was forbidden.

The civilian-military government repressed what should not be said, while at the same time instituting what should be said and therefore followed, practiced and legitimized. Hence the insistence and systematic effort to disseminate government propaganda and pronouncements. The works carried out by the National Press Department and signed by President Medici are part of this military government strategy. As we will see below, it is these speeches that create the visibility of a promising Brazil. The feeling of Brazil, the "love it or leave it", goes hand in hand with the triumphal rhetoric of Medici's speeches.

1.2   Speeches and policies of the military government

Medici's authorship authenticates the intentions of his government. An effect is created of which there would be no relevant practice that wasn't being said by his highest authority. This conclusion is allowed to me not only through the books of which Emilio Garrastazu Medici is the author. Alongside the published books are a

---

12 FICO, CARLOS. **Espionage, political policy, censorship and propaganda: the basic pillars of repression".** *In Republican Brazil. The time of the dictatorship. Military regime and social movements at the end of the 20th century. Vol. 4. Rio de Janeiro: Civilizaqao Brasileira, 2003.*

series of achievements and projects that corroborate the published speeches. The texts are linked to a systematic set of public policies that guarantee them. These pronouncements are accompanied by major government projects, such as the National Integration Plan, which articulates the construction of major highways and the insertion of agribusiness in the Amazon.

One of the ways for the population to get in touch with the government's political objectives is precisely through the words of the president himself. These words are no longer scattered throughout his speeches, but gathered together in text, published in a book. The president is no longer just the public figure in charge of the Brazilian state. He is also an author and, as such, he gives his speech a new commitment and authority.

In the case of President Medici's pronouncements, once they become published works, books, his words take on a new force and a more complex meaning. They move away from what is immediately consumable in order to be received in a certain way and which must, within society, be given a certain status. What the government does is establish, through the authorship attributed to the president, a certain group of discourses and their unique way of being. The works carry a certain regularity in what is being said, at the same time as the speeches are all linked to the projects and public policies of the military government between 1969 and 1974.

By choosing to study this period through a study of authorship, I have established some relationships that involve a certain way of thinking about history. It is important to state that the government's discourses are studied here in terms of their modes of existence. The sources are precisely those texts in which Medici is attributed the position of author. Therefore, I am not interested in looking at the concepts used by the president in the course of his texts - such as calling the military coup a "Revolution". The study of authorship contributes to understanding the way in which discourses are articulated in social relations. In other words, to propose the relevance of a study that problematizes the president as author is to see that this operation is linked to the way in which Brazilian society at the time appropriated the government's discourses and, for the most part, legitimized its policies. An author is not the origin of what is being said or written by him. Discourses are distributed in everyday life. Their practical dimension is precisely the way in which people reproduce these discourses in their daily lives. Therefore, when I talk about official discourses, I am aware that they do not originate in the state itself. They are cut up, regrouped, selected and ordered by this place of enunciation. It is precisely because they do not originate from the state, but reflect a series of social groups and classes, that Medici's pronouncements find the echo necessary for the exercise of his government.

This does not mean that, in the relationship between government and population, authorship is a condition for heads of state for a stable government relationship. In this study, I emphasize that the appropriation of discourses varies according to each culture and each specific historical moment - this is how it worked in Brazil in the early 70s.

The texts signed by Medici allow me to encircle the official speeches of the civil-military government. In this way, I consider that all the texts attributed to the president are themselves a set of objectives, goals and achievements of the dictatorship's government. The government's efforts to publish and distribute the texts authored by the president are associated with the need of a dictatorial government to guarantee the propagation of a unilateral discourse, while at the same time persecuting and censoring possible critics. However, the power that the texts exerted can only be measured when inserted into the set of achievements and practices of the government. By isolating authorship in order to think about the appropriation of these speeches, I can affirm that it is decisive for the status acquired by the pronouncements. The texts are surrounded by a notion of authority that only authorship can guarantee.

Another issue strengthens the notion of authority attributed to the president's pronouncements: the place of enunciation from which Medici delivers his speeches. This place is precisely the State. As I have been analyzing, Medici is not just an author; he is an author-president. This strengthens his arguments and gives them a double layer of truth and authority. As both author and president, his speeches are doubly shaped by institutional and juridical forms.

1.3 Medici: the invention of an author

Finally, I intend to detail the role of the government in the production of the speeches and the attribution of authorship to Medici. As I mentioned above, the notion of truth is intertwined with the notion of authority. The speeches of the military government are examples of this relationship between truth and authority. It is up to the state to make the calculations that will allow for better management of the population to be governed. The discourses that accompany governmental interdiction are therefore charged with truth. In other words, all of the president's pronouncements express the will to establish what is being said as true. This is because these speeches contain the intentions, objectives, projects and goals of the dictatorship's government between 1969 and 1974. If what the president says isn't taken as true, how can the military government's public policies be put into practice? Therefore, having the will to establish something that is taken as true is also assuming a will to interdict.

If truth is used as a path to interdiction, it also produces something artificial. Let's see. What President Medici is saying are arguments that are in line with the government's conception of national reality. This conception was far from being the only way of thinking about the direction of the country. Despite the 80% approval rating[13] , there was opposition and resistance to the government. There were other discourses and practices which, among other things, condemned the dictatorship's repression and its alliance with private capital. These opposition groups were on the side of truths other than those of the military government. Therefore, the opinions of the third government of the dictatorship did not involve the wishes of the whole of society, but we can conclude that at that time they became hegemonic. Because they were accepted as truth by the majority, it was the government's conceptions that shaped national reality. The Medici government's pronouncements do not manifest an absolute truth. But as soon as these were the speeches that articulated the military government's interdictions, all the pronouncements became hegemonically coated with truth.

---

[13]   REZENDE, 2001.

If truth produces something artificial, how can we think about authorship? The condition of author would itself be imbricated in the game of representations that constitute this artificiality. Once we accept that the dictatorship's set of speeches are articulated with its policies, we also accept that what is being said by the president does not only represent his conceptions. As discussed earlier, the pronouncements, like the dictatorship's policies, are made with the contribution of a series of "subject-positions" involved in the government's projects. The speeches refer to a series of social groups that made up the civil-military government. Just as truth is artificial, so is authorship. Medici is an invented author.

The person directly responsible for the military government's speeches between 1969 and 1974 was then its greatest authority. At first, there was nothing more obvious than holding the president responsible for the speeches of his government; or making the president the author of the government's pronouncements. But the study of authorship is not limited to understanding the attribution of a speech to an individual. The author exercises a link. Therefore, what interests me about the study of authorship does not form spontaneously as the attribution of a speech to an individual. It is a complex operation that constructs a certain being of reason called the author. Here, this being of reason goes by the name of Emilio Garrastazu Medici. The general is given the authority to talk about a series of problems, projects and solutions for the national reality. And when the same president becomes an author, he becomes an individual who in turn is deeply knowledgeable about the national reality. To this individual the population could entrust the fate of the country.

These are some of the characteristics that make the author a function. The intellectual effort that allows us to think about what an author is in our society, what makes him a function, is the same that allows us to understand the author as a fiction. In investigating the social and institutional mechanisms that resulted in the attribution of authorship to President Medici, the fragile relationship between the author and his work is exposed. Therefore, the l'una-author is not only a function, but also a lesson. The Medici author is an invention of the civilian military government.

2 THE DICTATORSHIP IN THE EARLY 1970S

2.1 Why Medici?

The study and research perspective adopted here carries with it a series of political intentions. History is not written without intentionality and in order to create a certain image of the Medici government and the dictatorship, I have mobilized political views of the past. The notion of perspective is not in itself an obstacle, but tends to become a meeting place, a public space where people can talk, discuss and discern[14]. This shared effort facilitates a historical understanding of Brazil in the early 1970s.

The Medici government is marked by ambiguity: on the one hand, violent repression and, on the other, recognized success in public opinion polls. But is the existence of a government that combines deliberate repression with popular recognition ambiguous? In the course of these lines is the answer to the question. Today, it is difficult to conceive of a government that uses unbridled violence and still manages to achieve high levels of legitimacy. Therefore, unraveling the idea of ambiguity in the Medici government is one of the aims of the book. The first step is to criticize the historiography of the period, since this ambiguity used to extend to historical research, but some recent perspectives have questioned this trait:

> Generally speaking, when studying the Medici government, attention tends to turn to two specific aspects: repression, which intensely affected armed opposition groups, leading to their almost absolute annihilation, and propaganda, which, according to common sense, was seductive, all-powerful, misleading, a veritable opium that numbed society in those years[15].

My study will focus neither on repression nor, in any case, on propaganda. I say in any case because it is possible to confuse public pronouncements and official

---

14 GINZBURG, Carlo. *Distance and perspective: two metaphors. In Wooden eyes: nine reflections on distance.* Sao Paulo: Companhia das Letras, 2001.
15 CORDEIRO, Janaina Martins. *Milagre, comemoraqdes e consenso ditatorial no Brasil,* 1972. *in* Confluenze Vol. 4, No. 2, 2012, pp. 82-102, ISSN 2036-0967, Dipartimento di Lingue, Letterature e Culture Moderne, Universita di Bologna.

speeches with government propaganda. However, I also share the view that propaganda is not an element loaded with misleading content, capable of deceiving people or getting them to do something they don't agree with. It is necessary to consider advertising as a mechanism capable of enhancing feelings and attitudes present in society itself. Advertising stimulates desires, it is not the epicenter of social discourses and practices. "The success of good advertising lies in its ability to engage in dialogue with values and traditions already ingrained in society."[16] .

When I adopt this perspective, I need to make it clear that I am entering territory that has been little explored by the historiography of the period. Between mistakes, successes and boldness, I intend to contribute to the understanding of the Medici government through some guiding questions, listed in Janaina Cordeiro's analysis:

> (...) I believe that the question 'Why Medici?' should be asked from other angles. Instead of denying his popularity, we should ask why he was so popular. What were the bases of his popularity? Can the propaganda-repression duo really explain everything? Finally, why did his popularity fade so quickly? Aren't the processes that resulted in the rapid rise of a president 'of few lights', the passions he was able to arouse and his rapid ostracism the keys to understanding the intense transformations that Brazilian society went through from the second half of the 1970s onwards?[17]

These are the paths I intend to follow in order to construct a historical interpretation. Distancing myself from the propaganda/repression pair is a way of creating a research problem capable of tackling the question of the legitimacy of the dictatorship. The attempt is to analyze the discourses and practices of the regime in order to investigate the government's rationality during the period. To this end, I chose to analyze some of the president's pronouncements at the beginning of the 1970s, as well as official documents that set out the goals and objectives of the dictatorship's third government. From the planning to the execution of public policies, it is possible

---

16 CORDEIRO, 2012, p.84. When I look at official discourses, I am aware that they do not originate in the state itself. They are cut out, regrouped, selected and ordered by this place of enunciation. It is precisely because they do not originate from the state, but are part of everyday life, that the government finds a channel of dialogue capable of winning society's adherence and not of deceiving it in its favor. FOUCAULT, Michel. *The Order of Discourse*. Edicoes Loyola, 2009.

17 CORDEIRO, Janaina. *Why remember? The collective memory of the Medici government and the dictatorship in Bage. In* REIS, Daniel Aarao; RIDENTI, Marcelo; MOTTA, Rodrigo Patto Sa (org.) *A ditadura que mudou o Brasil: 50 anos do golpe de 1964.* Rio de Janeiro: Zahar, 2014, p. 202.

to see the regime's attempt to build up its social bases, a condition for the establishment and maintenance of an authoritarian state. A problem of government is always a problem of legitimacy. Regardless of its success, the dictatorship had a project for the country that could only be implemented when the regime got closer to the population it governed. It was a process of conquest in which the strategy consisted of forging closer ties with certain social segments, proposing negotiations, bringing the government's intentions and the population's desires closer together, warding off questions and opposition. Having laid out the plot, the following text will analyze national integration policies. National integration is understood here as a fundamental issue in the rationale of the third government of the dictatorship. The need to integrate the country's regions guided much of the planning and execution of public policies during the period. National integration encompasses concerns about the size of the national territory and, in practice, means the implementation of government policies in rural areas of the country.

The Northeast and the Amazon emerged as key regions in the integration policies. Taken as a whole, these policies will be investigated alongside the government's attempt to build[18] society's adherence to the dictatorship's economic and political projects. Remembering that in order to investigate adherence to a particular government, it is also necessary to discuss resistance. Adherence presupposes resistance; compromises require escapes.

2.2 Governors and governed (Brazil - 1969/1974)

In analyzing Medici's speeches, I don't intend to look for what is hidden in the statements. In order to question the relationship between government and society, I have compiled arguments from the president's own speeches. The complexity of the research lies not in the attempt to reveal the hidden content of the words, but in the

---

18 MOTTA, Rodrigo Patto Sa. *As universidades e o regime militar: culturapolitica brasileira e modernizacao autoritaria.* Rio de Janeiro: Zahar, 2014. In this book, "adherence", "resistance" and "accommodation" are concepts used by the author to study the relationship between the dictatorship and universities. These concepts presuppose practices of support, confrontation or negotiation with the regime's authoritarian policies.

ability to articulate these statements to demonstrate the dictatorship's efforts in planning its public policies and building its social bases. The great challenge in problematizing the statements was not to repeat what was said in the official discourses. To articulate them but also to criticize them, without trying to reach the inner, hidden core of the words - the intention was never to reach the heart of a thought[15] . The government's calculations and reflections will be investigated in the dialog between public power and Brazilian society in the early 1970s:

> The unity of purpose between those who govern and those who are governed, the devotion of administrators and those who are administered to achieving the same ends, the efforts that one and the other expend, with selflessness and idealism, so that their legitimate expectations are not frustrated, strengthen the lakes of mutual trust between government authority and social forces, thus creating in our political framework a climate of stability, which allows us to look to the future with justified optimism[16] .

In his statement to his cabinet, the president defines "unity of purpose between the governors and the governed" as the key to political stability in the country. The general is aware that the success of his government depends on the trust established between the set of institutions and the governed population. This formula is what allows government to unfold without major turbulence. In his speech, Garrastazu Medici proposed an alliance with the governed. But in

15   FOUCAULT, Michel. The *Order of Discourse*. Edigoes Loyola, 2009.
16   President Medici. *The Sign of Tomorrow*. National Press Department, 1972, p. 111. Excerpt taken from the speech *"Impeto Criador" (Creative Impetus), delivered* on October 30, 1972 to the Ministerio do Governo. what terms can we think of such a union? The alliance between government and society is established in the confluence of interests, of purposes, as the president states above. Every negotiation presupposes an exchange, and it's no different between government and society. The confluence of interests is what allowed the dictatorship to carry out its political project for Brazil in the 1970s. However, social support for a given government cannot be measured solely by opinion polls or by the success of this or that public policy. In order to recover the dictatorship's ability to govern, or, to use a neologism, to write about its governability, it is necessary to recreate the political game between the government and the population. As Aarao Reis states:

In the differentiated range of attitudes that would contribute to the stability of the government and the country, it is also worth noting non-enthusiastic sympathy, benevolent neutrality, indifference or, at the limit, the feeling of absolute impotence. Zigzagging between them, with ambiguous or ambivalent attitudes, many wandered into undefined areas of penumbra, which one author called the gray zone At certain moments, it seemed that the government had managed to build a kind of consensus around itself, although the debate on the issue, and on the concept itself, still remains open[19] .

To begin with, we will investigate some of the mechanisms of adhesion, in other words, some of the elements that allow us to problematize the approximation between the government's intentions and social interests. In this game, society's intentions are presented as a kind of invariant. Individuals can be wrong about their personal interests, but they take the production of a collective interest as natural. The state is not expected to meet individual demands, but first to intervene in what is in the public interest. Therefore, it is in the appropriation of the general interest that individual purposes and desires are shaped. The production of the collective interest is therefore linked to individual desire. This is what marks out the naturalness of overall regulation and defines the artificiality of the means created to manage the population[20]

.

With regard to the dynamic between collective interest and individual desire, Medici states: "By modernizing society, as it has been doing, the current regime is introducing changes into the social body that enable individuals to take greater control of the direction of their own lives, in order to better satisfy their aspirations" (MEDICI, 1972, p. 111/112)[21] . *The* art consists of making people believe that the government is committed to fulfilling the interests of the population to the point of satisfying individual aspirations.

In this passage, another point should be highlighted. When Medici speaks, he is not referring exclusively to his mandate, that is, to the third government of the dictatorship. His words project the dictatorship as a whole. In this way, he carries with him the responsibility of a plan for the nation that doesn't begin with his government in October 1969, but which aims to continue a program that dates back to the 1964

---

19 REIS FILHO, Daniel Aarao. *Dictatorship and democracy in Brazil: from the 1964 coup to the 1988 Constitution.* Rio de Janeiro: Zahar, 2014.
20 FOUCAULT, Michel. *Security, Territory and Population.* Sao Paulo: Martins Fontes, 2008.
21 Excerpt also taken from the speech *"The creative impetus",* 1972. Quoted.

coup and which points to the democratic transition of the following years. These words bring me to another research challenge: to make General Medici's government unique among the governments of other generals who led the country's presidency during the dictatorship without, however, isolating it from the purposes that led the military to participate in a coup d'état in 1964.

The dictatorship steps in to safeguard order and democracy in Brazil. The coup ousted then president Joao Goulart and suspended the presidential elections. The regime, which included the Medici administration, is therefore characterized as a period of exception in national politics[22] . To the detriment of the political orientations of the pre-coup government, the dictatorship is associated, in official speeches, with the need to put into practice the capitalist modernization of the national economy and the security of Brazilian society from the dangers of communist subversion[23] . The exceptional nature of the dictatorship creates an effect of positivity around the regime's actions.

The urgency of national security and the break with the previous government's project did not limit the dictatorship's intentions as exclusively political. In the same pronouncement, made at a ministerial meeting, the president states that "due to its irrepressible dynamism, its eminently innovative nature, the revolutionary order established in 1964 cannot be defined as a simply political revolution"[24] . As the general president's rhetoric attests, the dictatorship came not only to block the Goulart government's political project, its basic reforms and its rapprochement with foreign communist governments[25] . Saying that the "revolution" was not simply political is a rhetorical device to affirm that the dictatorship regime brought with it a complete proposal for government management. New economic concepts, new social proposals. Understanding the dictatorship requires an analysis of all the political actions between

---

22 AGAMBEN, Giorgio. *State of exception.* Sao Paulo: Boitempo Editorial, 2004. For the discussion of what has come to be known as the "State of exception", I refer to Agamben's studies. The Italian philosopher considers the experience of totalitarian states in Europe. With due regard for the specifics, I use this reference to help understand authoritarianism in Brazil.

23 REIS FILHO, Daniel Aarao. *Military dictatorship, the left and society.* Zahar, 2000;

24   (MEDICI, 1972, p. 109)

25 FERREIRA, Marieta. *Joao Goulart: between memory and history.* Rio de Janeiro: Getulio Vargas Foundation-FGV, 2006.

1964 and 1985. Therefore, the study of the coup's motivations is not enough to end our understanding of the regime. Even if, over the years, the dictatorship's project has not been presented as a *continuum, in other* words, even if the dictatorship's directives contain ruptures and contradictions, even if over the years these directives have taken on new conlbnnations, it is important here to analyze the political machinery that allowed the generals to continue their governmental management, highlighting, as I said, the government of General Garrastazu Medici and the national integration works.

In order to guarantee the execution of its projects, a series of resources were used by the civil-military government. These resources do not point in a single direction, but always reinforce the attempt to define the regime as an intervention at the service of the Brazilian population. As the official speeches point out, the generals took power not just to establish a military order, but to show themselves to be at the service of a majority. Mindful of this commitment, Medici continues: "(...) given the immensity of the task to be accomplished, government action spreads, without loss of energy, into all the fields where its intervention is most urgent, in **order to**

to serve the collective interest"[26]

The insistence on defining the regime's government actions as guided by the collective interest is a way of building the dictatorship's legitimacy. Achieving this legitimacy requires the support of a large part of the governed population. What I mean is that the problem of legitimacy is a problem of the majority. If a certain social group occupies public power, it does so with the backing of a majority. The idea of the majority, and consequently that of the minority, belongs to the universe of political thought - and Medici's speeches do not escape these limits. By defending the collective interest, the government enters the dispute for the representation of the majority and imposes on the people a confrontation in terms of quantity. What I want to problematize, however, is the way in which this general interest is also an invention. It is the institutions and official discourses that produce the collective interest and define what is good for the majority. And the richer everyone's interest is,

---

[26] MEDICI, 1972, p. 110, emphasis added.

the poorer and more expropriated everyone's interest is. It was in the name of society, of the collective, of the nation, that the dictatorship government found enough support to put into practice a whole range of authoritarian policies, including violence and torture imposed on a political minority. Demonstrating the confluence between the production of a collective interest and the government's interest is a path of analysis that puts society back in the position of being responsible for the government that intends to administer it. The coup was not a bolt from the blue and the generals cannot be the only ones to answer for the atrocities of the period.[27]

On the same occasion that he addresses his ministers, General Medici outlines some strategies for getting closer to society:

> the consensus of the different social classes, which have never refused to support the government's measures as a whole, or, in other words, in the applause of public opinion, the regime finds a touchstone of legitimacy in the direction our public life has taken[28] .

According to the then president, support for this or that government measure, or the consent of what he calls "public opinion", are key issues in the government's conquest of legitimacy in the 1970s. But what is most striking in this passage is the use of the idea of consensus: "in the consensus of the different social classes (...) the regime finds a touchstone of legitimacy". When the official speech uses this category, it points to the need for the state to embrace a differentiated set of social behaviors and attitudes. Paraphrasing the work of Janaina Cordeiro[29] , I bring the definition of this concept according to the *Dicionario de Politica*[30] :

> The term consensus denotes the existence of an agreement between the members of a given social unit regarding principles, values, norms, as well as the objectives sought by the community and the means to achieve them. Consensus is therefore expressed in the existence of beliefs that are more or less shared by the members of a society[31] .

Consensus becomes a crucial concept for debating the political stability of the

---

27 REIS FILHO, 2014.
28 MEDICI, 1972, p. 111.
29 CORDEIRO, Janaina. *The dictatorship in times of miracle: celebrations, pride and consent*. Rio de Janeiro: Editora FGV, 2015.
30 BOBBIO, Norberto. MATTEUCCI, Nicola; PASQUINO, Gianfranco. *Dictionary of Politics,* 1998.
31 BOBBIO; et. Al, 1998, p. 240.

regime. I say that consensus does and *does* not *become* a fundamental concept for investigating the legitimacy of the dictatorship. This *is* because consensus only becomes a crucial element for investigating the legitimacy of the dictatorship when it appears in official discourses. We cannot take the idea of consensus as a natural political process. In other words, the idea of consensus is itself a discursive production of the dictatorship. Consensus does not exist as a target to be achieved by government measures, much less is it something given to be measured by public opinion polls. It is not a goal, but a production that creates the effect of national unity. Consensus does not exist a priori, as a political category capable of clearly describing social behavior and the relationship between a government and a governed population. In short, consensus cannot be achieved by decree. We have seen on previous pages that there was a wide range of attitudes towards the dictatorship, zigzags, ambiguities and ambivalences[32] . In the same way that repression cannot be the key to understanding the legitimacy of the dictatorship, neither can consensus alone explain why the generals remained in power. Taken in isolation, the concept carries a generalizing and misleading content. However, when it appears in Medici's speech, it is this very effect that the president wants to create. Consensus is a discursive effect used by the Medici government. By using it, the president created the false idea of agreement around his government measures. In this agreement, the heterogeneity of the social body is left in the background and individuals grant a certain government proposal the responsibility of also leading their lives. For those who occupy the seats of public power, the attempt is to create unity around the government's commitment.

In the same speech that talks about consensus, I also highlight the way in which social classes and legitimacy are articulated. "In the consensus of the different social classes, (...) the regime finds a touchstone of legitimacy *(...)"[33]* . On the occasions when the dictatorship's government uses the notion of social classes, its intention is always to avoid conflict between these groups. The idea that society is divided into classes is marked by conflict between the parties and not by the unity of their interests. In order to maintain order and avoid revolt, social classes are mobilized as a

---

32 REIS FILHO, 2014.

33 MEDICI, 1972. Cited.

demonstration that the government is willing to respond to the interests of each social segment. In the government's rhetoric, conflict has given way to consensus. But there is no consensus between antagonistic social groups.

It's not always the case that the official speeches I've had the opportunity to see will deal with society as divided into social classes. This will depend on a number of factors, such as the timing of the president's speech. It all depends on the effect Medici wants to create. Therefore, it is sometimes more appropriate to understand society as a body in which there are no divisions by class, color or gender. When talking about the population without using these social cut-outs, it is common to use generalizing notions such as nagao, Brazilian people, etc. It must be made clear that in recovering these official speeches I don't always intend to point out a kind of coherence in the president's words that would allow me to create a regularity or unity around the dictatorship's policies. In my contact with these speeches, I realize that they often cancel each other out, correct each other and compensate for each other[34].

For the government, it is not important to reinforce differences, but to forge policies within which we perceive ourselves as equals. This equality manifests itself in the hope that the government will make our lives better. Collective desires and aspirations create the farce of an equal society. Therefore, and it is essential to say this, the idea that there is unity around the social body is a path to government interdiction. Unity homogenizes, reduces conflicts, hides differences, conceals dominance and masks oppression.

Finally, the importance of discussing consensus does not lie in pointing out the existence of a general agreement between the government and Brazilian society in the 1970s. I believe that investigating the construction of legitimacy involves the challenge of understanding the conformation of its support and social bases. When referring to the dictatorship in Brazil, Aarao Reis states that:

> Overall, the attitudes that make up the consensus built under dictatorships prevailed: alongside pure and simple adherence, conformism in the face of what is considered irreversible, fear of reprisals, a feeling of powerlessness, uncompromising sympathy or, at the limit, indifference. Not to mention the

---

34 FOUCAULT, 2009.

Despite the relevance of these studies, I don't intend to analyze in detail the different attitudes and behaviors towards the policies of the dictatorial regime. The task of this text is to expose the discursive strategy used by the third government of the dictatorship in order to problematize its governmental rationality. To continue this analysis, I have selected some speeches dealing with the planning and execution of public policies in the early 1970s. The field of public policies is vast and here I will focus on national integration policies. Integration was a presupposition of the Medici government and marked the way in which this general dealt with the problems of two regions of the national territory - the Northeast and the Amazon.

2.3 The military didn't rule alone

The value of Medici's pronouncements increases when we realize that they were intended to be an important channel for dialogue between the dictatorship and the population, as well as presenting some of his government's political strategies and alliances. Many of these official speeches were broadcast nationally on radio and television. Below, I have selected some excerpts from speeches made by Garrastazu Medici in the first quarter of 1970. As it was the beginning of his government, these speeches expose some of the circumstances that made Medici president of Brazil. Problematizing Medici's speeches implies describing the historical moment in which the president was inserted, taking up the particularities of the period in which he responded as head of government.

By recovering these pronouncements, it is possible to identify some segments of society that participated in and/or supported the dictatorship government. President Medici was a general, but his speeches were not only made from a military perspective. Seeing in the pronouncements the support of certain subjects and institutions is a way of pointing to the thesis that the formation of the dictatorship

---

35 REIS FILHO, 2014, p. 118.

government involved significant civilian participation.

In order to analyze the policies of national integration, which is the objective guiding the writing of the following chapters, I consider it essential to discuss the negotiations that guided the exercise of government at the beginning of the 1970s. In other words, which social segments allied themselves with the Brazilian rulers of the time? Identifying with whom the generals governed is one way of understanding the objectives of their governmental practice.

On the occasion of the sixth anniversary of the dictatorship, Medici said on radio and television:

> The inspiring force of the Margo Revolution comes from the Alleluia lights, in the symbolism of resurrection and rebirth. The revolutionaries of the first hour felt this force within themselves, understanding that the light of Easter dilutes the shadow of Calvary. The future of Brazil demands that those who later accepted the Revolution, those who finally recognized its services, or those who only understood or were inclined towards it, have the greatness to see it as the beginning of a new era.[36]

This discourse reveals how the government appropriated images and representations from the Catholic Christian tradition to reinforce its defense of the dictatorship that had been installed in Brazil. In the early hours of April 1, 1964, the coup that ousted President Joao Goulart and installed General Castelo Branco as the country's president took place. It was Easter time, an important moment in the Christian calendar. In this pronouncement, Medici took advantage of the coincidence between the dates to link the coup d'état, which they call the "Revolution"[37], with the inauguration of a new era which, at Easter, is linked to the resurrection. In Medici's words, the regime was inaugurating a new era in Brazilian history. It was salvation for the country. Compared to the time of resurrection and rebirth, the dictatorship was a kind of national redemption.

As mentioned earlier, this statement was made on April 1, 1970, on the occasion of the sixth anniversary of the military coup in 1964. In 1970, the anniversary of the dictatorship followed the Easter celebrations, which in the Brazilian calendar is an important national holiday. In a country with a Catholic majority,

---

36 MEDICI, 1970, p. 93.
37 On the concept of Revolution, see KOSELLECK, Reinhart. *Future Past: Contribution to the Semantics of Historical Times.* Pontifical Catholic University of Rio de Janeiro, 2006.

Easter is a time of Christian commotion that did not escape the dictatorship's uses and comparisons. In this speech, the president was addressing the Brazilian population as a whole, all social classes. Using the vocabulary of Christian symbolism was a way of "speaking the language of the people". Comparing the regime to Easter was a way of facilitating communication between the government and the population.

The use of the comparison between the inauguration of the dictatorship and the symbolism of resurrection and rebirth is not restricted to a rhetorical resource used by the general president during the sixth anniversary of the regime. This comparison also takes us back to the time of the coup and the alliance between the military and the Catholic Church. Without the unity of the conservative segments, it would have been impossible to oust the then president Joao Goulart. In another passage from the same speech, the general comments on the formation of this conservative bloc:

> The nation remembers the Lent of 1964, sadder for us than any other, because then the democratic and Christian values of the Brazilian soul were crucified in the siege of disorder and turmoil, injustice, demagoguery and intimidation, which was to end on the tormenting Friday the 13th. The march of the family through the streets, of the Christian religious sentiment of our people, demanding an end to all the excesses, is alive and well in the country's memory[38] .

The "march of the family", to which Medici refers, is the March of the Family with God for Freedom[39] . These marches were street demonstrations that spread across the country in 1964. Among the marches, two deserve to be highlighted. The first, in the city of Sao Paulo, took place on March 19, 1964, a few days before the generals took over the presidency. On that day, the people of São Paulo who marched in the streets of the capital demanded political intervention to stop the subversive threats to Christian-Catholic morality. The second march, in Rio de Janeiro, was a consecration to the coup and also became known as *The Victory March,* held the day after the military intervention - April 2, 1964. The *victory march* was an act that "celebrated the success of the coup and celebrated the downfall of Jango and the forces favorable to reforms and the popular national-statist project."[40] . Both marches were attended by

---

38 MEDICI, 1970, p. 87.

39 PRESOT, Aline Alves. *The marches of the family with God for freedom and the military coup of 1964.* Master's thesis, Postgraduate Program in History, UFRJ, Rio de Janeiro, 2004.

40 In an article published in August 2012 - *O sol sem peneira (The sun without a sieve),* Daniel Araao Reis argues that the support of civil society was fundamental to the long life of the military dictatorship in

hundreds of thousands of people. Both demonstrations brought together the conservative sectors of Brazilian society. These segments felt threatened by the possibility of the Goulart government carrying out a radical transformation of Brazilian society. In general, the subversive threats were seen in the political reforms proposed by the then president and in his rapprochement with countries like China and the Soviet Union[41]. For a large part of the population, the reforms were radical and represented subversion. Rumors grew of the rise of a popular government with communist influences. The rumors also propagated the dangers that communism offered to the Church, the family, morals and the good customs of the Christian population[42]. And if the repression of communism in Brazil always comes with a moralizing content, it was no different in the *"March 31 Revolution"* movement[43]. The military shared the views of the Christian and conservative groups who took to the streets in the Marches of the Family with God for Freedom. Throughout the regime, these segments and religious institutions were important support sectors for the authoritarianism of the Brazilian government during the dictatorship.

Medici's pronouncements attest to the fact that the dictatorship continued to use Christian groups during the 1970s. Mobilizing Christian representations in official speeches was a way for the dictatorship to expose its alliance with part of the Catholic Church. A fundamental point in the alliance between part of the Catholic Church, the Evangelical Churches and the Brazilian state in the 1970s was the ability of religious institutions to mediate a set of values dear to the authoritarian government of the dictatorship[44]. The rapprochement between the values propagated by both the Church

---

Brazil. For the author, one of the greatest expressions of civil participation were the marches in support of the coup. The movement that became known as A Marcha da Familia com Deus pela Liberdade had the direct support of the CNBB - National Conference of Bishops of Brazil. This article is a historiographical milestone in defining the dictatorship as a civil-military government. Daniel Araao Reis is a professor at Fluminense Federal University and the author of *Military Dictatorship, Lefts and Society* (Zahar, 2000).

41 BARRETO, Tulio & FERREIRA, Laurindo (eds). *On the trail of the coup: 1964 revisited.* Recife: A fundagao; Editora Massangana, 2012.

42 MONTEGRO, Antonio. *Historia e Memoria de Lutas Politicas* in Marcas da Memoria: Historia Oral da Amistia no Brasil. Recife: Ed. Universitaria da UFPE, 2012.

43 MOTTA, Rodrigo Patto Sa. *On guard against the "red danger": anti-communism in Brazil, 19171964.* Perspectiva Publishing House, 2002.

44 The Catholic Church supported the 1964 coup, but after 1968, some sectors of the institution, linked to the influences of "Liberation Theology", began to carry out a series of social works, both in the city and in the countryside, fighting for the rights of the poorest segments of Brazil. Priests, bishops, nuns and lay

and the State facilitated popular adherence to the dictatorship's policies.

Therefore, order and government control are guaranteed by an articulated network of institutions. The state, the church and the family, for example, play an important role in proposing rules and behaviors to individuals and social groups. Once articulated, these institutions fostered the insertion and reproduction of conservative ideals and practices in the daily life of Brazilian society in the early 1970s.

Another partner of the military was the private sector, a group of national and international companies that participated in the dictatorship's government projects. These entrepreneurs and corporations were always supported by the government, whether in the countryside or in the city[45] . In the managers' view, capitalist development can only be achieved through the union of private enterprise and government enterprise. In Medici's words, it is possible to visualize the union between State and private initiative:

> I would therefore like to define the national objectives that I consider to be my government's priorities. First of all, I want to focus our efforts on achieving an accelerated and sustainable pace of development. I want this development effort to be compatible with internal stability and security. And I will seek to achieve this development and security by building a politically open society that reconciles the need to maintain the acceleration of development with the maintenance of freedoms and **the greatest possible degree of privatization and decentralization of economic power.** [46]

In these words are some of the economic and political commitments of the dictatorship at the time of its third government. Capitalist development requires economic dynamism in which financial and industrial agents multiply.

---

people inspired by liberation theology were persecuted as communists (MONTENEGRO, 2010).

45 In her book entitled *A lenda do ouro verde: politico de colonizaçao no Brasil contemporaneo (The legend of green gold: colonization policy in contemporary Brazil.* fUNICEM Publications, 2002), Regina Beatriz proposes a study of the proximity of agro-industry entrepreneurs to the politics of the dictatorship. According to the author, this alliance was fundamental to the policy of colonizing the Amazon and the Brazilian Midwest. The dictatorship government gave businessmen a free pass so that they could exploit land and labor in the region. By recovering trajectories and testimonies, the author points out the mechanisms of this political-business alliance. She also recovers some of the practices used by these businessmen to establish a regime of capitalist exploitation in the countryside. Businessmen and the military were confused when it came to exploiting and repressing workers in the region. The book offers us a "microhistorical" view of colonization policy and is an important reference for this methodology in the approach to colonization policies in contemporary Brazil. By bringing the magnifying glass closer, it is possible to capture a series of practices and mechanisms of the political-business alliance that would go unnoticed in the eyes of a more general history.

46 MEDICI, 1970, p. 65, emphasis added.

Note that the development effort propagated by Medici appears to be linked to security and stability. Modernizing capitalism and guaranteeing national security are two pillars of the dictatorship's third government. But I've emphasized in this passage that development and national security would be achieved with "the greatest possible degree of privatism and decentralization of economic power". Privatizing services and institutions and decentralizing economic power is a way of inviting private initiative to participate in your government. The economy would then be a territory to be co-managed with entrepreneurs. During the dictatorship, the private sector held public positions and actively participated in the government, which earned them high levels of profitability[47] . The composition of the dictatorship's government had the support and participation of the private sector, a group that held the power of acquisition, a rich and privileged minority in Brazilian society.

In national integration policies, private initiative was a determining factor in the occupation of the Amazon from the 1970s onwards. In order to establish agribusiness in the region, the dictatorship granted tax incentives that made it easier for landowners to acquire land. Later on, we will see that according to the speeches of Garrastazu Medici and other spokespeople for his government, only big businessmen were capable of guaranteeing the modernization of agricultural production in rural Brazil.

Being on the side of private initiative was a position that kept the regime committed to the development of the capitalist system and, consequently, well away from communist proposals. During the 1970s, capitalism and communism were models of economic management that rivaled for influence around the globe. In the communist experiment, the economy was managed with a minimum degree of privatization. Economic management was reserved for the state and its institutions.

In another official speech, when comparing different economic policy proposals, General Medici confronts these two economic models, the capitalist and the communist:

> Prosperity or economic growth has therefore become an essential element in

---

47 DREIFUSS, Rene. Armand. 1964: the conquest of the State. *Petropolis: Vozes,* 1981. In this book, the author lists the companies that took part in the government's projects and the businessmen who occupied the seats of public power during the dictatorship.

achieving collective well-being. It would really be against common sense for anyone to want to distribute goods in ever greater proportions if they didn't grow at the same rate.[48]

According to the Medici government's economic policy, eternalized in the phrase of the then Finance Minister, it was necessary to *"make the cake grow and then divide it up"*. Heat up the economy, accelerate growth and develop the country and then deal with the problem of income distribution. In this formula, anyone who defended the immediate distribution of goods and criticized land concentration was an enemy of the dictatorship. In common sense, social justice and the distribution of goods "are communist things". Therefore, for the military government, the sin of "distributing goods" was committed by those people identified with the need for radical reforms in Brazilian society - the subversives. In the conservative view shared and disseminated by the Brazilian government at the time, communists, in other words, subversives, were seen as enemies of order, morality and the well-being of the Brazilian people. It's hard to believe that every individual who, among other factors, believed in the need for reform and/or criticized the dictatorship regime was necessarily a communist militant, in this case, a "subversive". However, in general, the discourse that criticized the property regime and land concentration in the country was carried out by organizations and movements resisting the dictatorship and capitalism, therefore communist or socialist organizations. It was these same organizations that also propagandized the need for an immediate distribution of property. However, the organizations resisting the dictatorship were not homogeneous either and should be thought of as a range of different initiatives[49]. However, they all made up the diffuse field that today we call the "left"

When the generals took over the presidency, the military took over the reins of the Brazilian government.[50] In the face-to-face confrontation with the left, the dictatorship used military force to guarantee the security of its government. The independence enjoyed by the military led not only to abuses of power, but also to acts that led to the creation of a violent and inhumane apparatus. The generals spared no

---

48 MEDICI, 1970, p. 48.
49 ARAUJO, Maria Paula Nascimento. *Fragmented Utopia: the new left in Brazil and the world in the 1970s*. FGV Editora, 2000. Reis Filho, Daniel Aarao. *Military dictatorship, lefts and society*. Zahar, 2000.
50 REIS FILHO, 2014.

effort or consequences to eradicate political opposition to the dictatorship. There was no control, supervision or regulation of military activity outside the army, navy or air force. The military was the law itself. In this sense, it is unquestionable that the authoritarianism of the dictatorship was largely linked to the military profile of that government. The military didn't rule alone, but its permanence was fundamental to the continuity of a dictatorial regime.

General Garrastazu Medici's speeches also valued the role of the armed forces in his government. In the following excerpt, the president pays tribute to the agents of repression:

> And here I stand in solidarity with all those who, in anonymity and at the risk of their own lives, as unjustified agents of this country's security, face open defiance, violence, the liberation of instincts and disrespect for the law. Thanks to their sacrifices, we are overcoming the terrorism of a minority deceived by the fallacy of systems of life that are incompatible with the character of our people and we can already glimpse the total normalization of national life.[51]

The action of the national security agents was justified by the "normalization of national life". According to the president, the military confronted the armed violence of left-wing groups, already identified as *terrorists, at the* risk of their own lives. On the other hand, the practices of resistance appear to be associated with the "liberation of instincts" and "disrespect for the law". Repression is therefore legitimized by its moralizing content. In Medici's words, the left appear as minorities deceived by "systems of life incompatible with the character of our people". These systems corresponded to the communist way of life. In order to guarantee the development of capitalism in Brazil and to safeguard the conservative morals of "our people", security was needed that only the military could be responsible for. In this sense, during the 1970s, the defense of capitalism was the security of maintaining conservative moral standards. The defense of conservative morality justified the authoritarianism of the military intervention.

The legitimacy of any relationship of authority is based on the sense of security carried by the oppressor. This understanding makes it easier to criticize the social foundations of the dictatorship and especially of the Medici government. Security is a

---

51 MEDICI, 1970, p. 80.

feeling without which we cannot imagine the reasons that made the generals the presidents of Brazil between the 1960s and 1980s. Even though it committed the abuses and atrocities of repression, the dictatorship's police regime was officially justifiable when it was linked to a need to secure the governed population and safeguard social order.

However, the participation of the military in the government is also exalted in official pronouncements, fulfilling a function other than guaranteeing security for the Brazilian population. In other speeches, the military character of a president is valued because of the moral conduct of his upbringing:

> I have based my conduct on the basic principles that comrades know and practice: **respect for authority, firmness of purpose, authenticity, clarity of attitude, austerity, discipline and hierarchy**. In reciprocity, I am aware that all my attitudes and determinations as Commander-in-Chief will have the full correspondence of my commanders, within the rigor of the institutional norms that govern us all.[52]

These are some of the principles of military conduct that, according to Medici himself, made up his posture as president. In other words, rather than exalting the general's character, these values guided the exercise of his government. Authority, discipline and hierarchy... these words denote some of the characteristics that marked Medici's way of governing. Respect for authority is a principle of the military career, just as the dictatorship ruled in an authoritarian manner. Repression and censorship are characteristics of an authoritarian government and have accompanied the years of the regime since the 1964 coup. Discipline, another behavior valued in a military career, is a requirement of order. For example, only with discipline is it possible to maintain a docile life and keep away from moral slips. It has also been pointed out that the fight against the dictatorship was also associated with transgressing the moral values of Brazilian society. Discipline was therefore encouraged as a way of proposing and enforcing the morals of a conservative society. Finally, hierarchy is also another principle without which military organization cannot function. In the experience of the dictatorship, hierarchy can be linked to the federal centralization of the regime's political command and control. The duties of the commander and chief of

---

52 MEDICI, 1970, p. 30, emphasis added.

the nation had to be respected and fulfilled. The general president closed the national congress whenever he wanted, just as during some years of the regime he appointed governors and mayors around the country. The political guidelines of the Brazilian state were centralized in the federal government. The dictators ruled by decree. Even though the participation of other social segments and individuals was decisive in the execution of public policies, everyone had to respect the hierarchy and obey the generals' final word. Authoritarianism, discipline and hierarchy are qualities that can be associated with any dictatorial government or military regime. However, it was Emilio Garrastazu Medici's own words that authorized the discussion of the Brazilian case. His speeches make the dictatorship in Brazil between the 1960s and 1980s unique.

Whatever the real scope of their words, these pronouncements propose rules of conduct. In order to propose and encourage behavior, the speeches establish a kind of upward and downward continuum[53] . In the upward movement, official speeches appropriate qualities valued by common sense to build the profile of a given government. Valuing military training in a president's career, and making the case that a head of government must be disciplined, firm and commanding, know how to control his impulses and pleasures - "he who governs the state must first know how to govern himself, govern his family, his property, his patrimony"[54] . The downward movement is the way in which the government starts to encourage certain rules of conduct among the population it governs. If the president is capable of being a good ruler, it's up to individuals to control themselves, to be good rulers. This is descending continuity "in the sense that, when the state is well governed, parents know how to govern their children".
families, their property, their assets... "[55] .The upward and downward movement of the techniques of government, resulting from the pact between institutions and the governed, create the success of the social order advocated by the dictatorship.

---

53 FOUCAULT, Michel. *Microphysics of Power.* Organized and translated by Roberto Machado. Rio de Janeiro: Edigoes Graal, 1984.
54 FOUCAULT, 1984, p 281.

---

55 FOUCAULT, 1984, p 281.

During the dictatorship, concern about General Medici's conduct seems to me to be central to the problem of legitimacy. The president who ruled the country between 1969 and 1974 adopted an authoritarian stance, linked to the discipline and hierarchy of military conduct. According to Elio Gaspari, General Garrastazu Medici

> He presided over the country in silence, reading speeches written by others, without social gatherings, ruthless with gossip. He passed through public life with scrupulous personal honor. From the presidency he took a salary of Cr$3439.98 net per month (equivalent to 72 dollars) and nothing more. He postponed an increase in meat prices in order to sell the oxen from his ranch at low prices and diverted the traffic from a road so that it wouldn't increase the value of his land. His wife decorated the official farm in Riacho Fundo with used furniture collected from the civil service warehouses in Brasilia[56].

All the pronouncements that have appeared so far in this text are precisely the speeches read by the general during the period of his government. Whether or not he actually wrote them doesn't matter. What is relevant to the discussion I am presenting here is that these speeches were collected and published during the years of his government and, above all, that the authorship of all of them was attributed to Garrastazu Medici. It's hard to believe that the general president was solely responsible for the texts, as well as for their subsequent editing and publication. But all the books and almost all the speeches that make up the collection of his pronouncements between 1969 and 1974 are signed by President Medici. The authorship of the speeches is attributed exclusively to the general.

The posture, personality and conduct of a general president cannot be taken for granted. A public figure's identity is constructed to achieve certain ends. The conduct presented to us above constructs the image of a simple, honest man. These images carry the idea of a president of the people, an ordinary man like most, honest and willing to work. Encouraging this behavior in a head of nation or choosing a general with these characteristics as president is a strategy to bring the president closer to the people he governs.

In the case of Garrastazu Medici, his choice to occupy the post of president, as well as the process that built up a certain profile of ruler, responded to the

---

56 GASPARI, 2012, p. 136

particularities of the historical moment that the dictatorship was going through. Medici took over the presidency in October 1969. The previous president, General Costa e Silva, had left office for health reasons. The general's condition was serious when he left office - he was suffering from paralysis as a result of what was diagnosed as a stroke[57] . With Costa e Silva's unexpected departure, the dictatorship had to face a troubled time. His vice-president, Pedro Aleixo, did not take over the position left vacant by his running mate, which suggests that he was not considered a trustworthy person by the upper echelons of the armed forces; after all, he was a civilian, a career politician who had never held a post in the military. A military junta was formed to replace Costa e Silva, made up of three officers: Aurelio de Lira Tavares, Minister of the Army; Admiral Augusto Rademaker[58] , Minister of the Navy; and Brigadier Marcio de Sousa e Melo, Minister of Aeronautics. The junta remained in office from August 31, 1969 to October 30, 1969. On that day, General Garrastazu Medici took office.

During the months in which the military junta remained in power, the dictatorship no longer had a single public figure to represent the government and allow the image of the nation's political leader to be advertised. The entry of a new general president was accompanied by the need to exploit his personal and political identity. In Medici's case, we see a process in which the construction of a figure with a firm hand, sympathetic to the profile of the nation's common man, stands out.

2.4 Natural elements and their transformation: the *golden years and the leaden years*

Today, the Medici government is hegemonically known as the "leaden years" of the dictatorship. Another denomination that for a long time marked the image of the period was to identify the first half of the 1970s as the "golden years" of the regime.

---

57 AGOSTINHO, Gilberto. *Soccer and the Military Dictatorship in Brazil.* Nossa Historia magazine, no. 14, December 2004.

58 Rademaker was personally chosen by Medici as vice president of his government. According to journalist Elio Gaspari, there was a certain amount of distrust on the part of the Armed Forces for the Admiral to occupy the position of vice president. In view of this, General Medici did not give up his choice and made Rademaker's vice-presidency a condition for him to take over as head of the government in Brasilia. From then on, the general would have said that this stance was decisive in guaranteeing his authority at the helm of government (GASPARI, 2002).

At the beginning I said that the study of the Medici government is marked by two main strands. The first focuses on repression during the first half of the 1970s. To this end, the censorship, persecution, assassinations and torture that marked the years in which the president of the republic went by the name of Garrastazu Medici are revisited. The second strand focuses on government propaganda, traditionally identified as the main vehicle for gaining the support of the Brazilian population at the time. In general, we can consider that the historiographical narrative that privileged repression contributed to the construction of the image of the "years of lead". On the other hand, propaganda studies reinforce the idea of the "golden years", since Aerp (Special Public Relations Agency)[59] used the "Brazilian miracle" and economic growth to build a positive image of the authoritarian government. The two perspectives differ in their understanding of the period: the gold one emphasizes the "super-powerful" propaganda, associated with the dictatorship's deceitful action around the practices of its government; the lead one privileges repression and conceives the period as marked by the regime's violence. However, these two perspectives end up approaching each other when the intention is to place society in a position of victim of the dictatorship; either deceived by propaganda or crushed by deliberate repression.

At this point it's natural to ask: how can such different images - gold and lead - make up the vision of the same historical period? On the one hand, the "golden years", a belief in development, the Brazilian miracle and the country's economic modernization; on the other, the years of lead, which take us back to a society marked by conflict, torture, repression and censorship of freedom of expression. The possible contradiction between these antagonistic denominations can be better problematized when investigated through a study of government rationality and the agendas that accompany it.

But in the analyses that follow, the terms "years of lead" and/or "golden years" lose the centrality that memory and historiography have given them. These terms are important to me insofar as they make it possible to debate development and national

---

59 An institution created by the Medici government, it was responsible for government propaganda in the early 1970s.

security policies. From now on, the golden years will be dealt with in the universe of economic policies, just as the years of lead will be problematized through national security agendas:

> On the one hand, we will have a whole series of mechanisms that are part of the economy, that are part of the management of the population and whose function will be to increase the strength of the state and, on the other hand, a certain apparatus or a certain number of instruments that will ensure that disorder, irregularities, illegality and delinquency are prevented or repressed.[60]

The attempt is to show that the characterization of the Medici government as "years of lead" or "years of gold" refers to historical events that allow us to visualize the way in which government reason conceives and executes its public policies. First "golden years", then "years of lead" - these denominations emerge from the arbitrariness that constitutes the attempt to establish a single meaning for a given period in Brazilian history.

The "golden years" and the "years of lead" are also linked to the government's objectives with the National Integration Program. The alliance with private enterprise and the stimulation of agro-industry in the countryside were factors that contributed to economic growth and the consequent feeling that we were living through the "golden years" of national history. The occupation of the frontiers and the stimulation of the displacement of labor from the Northeast will also be presented as strategies for controlling the political order in Brazil in the 1970s. Before delving into the universe of integration policies and their main project, the PIN, other historical conditions in which the third government of the dictatorship was inserted will be problematized.

2.4.1 The Brazilian Miracle

In 1970, government planning aimed to accelerate economic growth during Medici's years as president. This rate was initially set at between 7% and 9% per year, tending to rise to 10% over the course of Medici's administration[61] . According to the Ministry of Planning, "The realization of this goal will place Brazil among the fastest

---

60 FOUCAULT, Michel. *Security, Territory and Population.* Sao Paulo: Martins Fontes, 2008, p. 475.
61 Data available at: MINISTRY OF PLANNING. *Goals and Bases for Government Action.* National Press Department, 1970, p. 16.

growing countries in the world in recent times"[62] . These are some of the indices that characterize the economic miracle. What they actually meant for the economy is not worth discussing at this point. In speeches, by presenting the growth of economic indices, the government is able to attest to the development of Brazilian society, its progress towards the level of industrialized countries. By manipulating economic indices, the state and its institutions justify government intervention[6364] .

The economy is the field in which the government forges the language of planning and executing its public policies. The constitution of government knowledge, governability, involves the economy and processes relating to the population, more precisely, an economy of the population. The relationship between the population and the territory - its things and wealth - constitutes what we call political economy, a type of intervention that is characteristic of contemporary forms of government. In the 16th century, the term economy referred to a form of government; in the 18th century, it refers to a level of reality, a field of intervention[62] . Economics and politics come together to form the arts of governing; a regime that affects the population[65] .

The development of the economy was a goal of the Medici government. The growth in economic indices during those years led to the term "Brazilian miracle" being coined. But in order to understand the consequences of the idea that the country was going through a miraculous period, we must think of discourses as statements that are capable of articulating what we think, say and do as historical events. Therefore, the appearance of the term "Brazilian miracle" in the national political sphere mobilized the population in terms of their conception and feelings about the Medici

---

62 MINISTRY OF PLANNING. *Metas e Bases para Acao de Governo*. Taking the studies of Aarao Reis as a reference and cross-referencing them with the data available in the official document, I can affirm that the goals seem not only to have been met, but surpassed. According to the author, "the upward swing of the figures was impressive, and still is today, as the country has never again achieved such high results: 9.5% in 1970, 11.3% in 1971; 10.4% in

At the top was industry, with rates of 14% per year, especially the locomotives of the process: the automobile industry, the electronics industry and the construction industry, with rates of over 20% per year (AARAO REIS, 2014, p. 79)."

63 "By this word, 'governmentality', I mean the whole of the institutions, the procedures, analyses and reflections, calculations and tactics that make it possible to exercise a very specific, albeit very complex, form of power whose main target is the population, whose main form of knowledge is political economy, and whose essential technical instrument is the security apparatus (FOUCAULT, 2008, p. 143)".

62 FOUCAULT, 2008.

government, and was an important factor in convincing society of the dictatorship's guidelines.

The entry "Brazilian miracle" first appeared in Jornal do Brasil on May 12, 1970. I chose this newspaper, among other factors, because it represented a vehicle of support for the dictatorship. In other words, if the miracle is linked to the success of that government, it's hard to imagine that a newspaper that supports the dictatorship would miss the chance to report on it. Thus, on the front page of May 12, 1970, a Tuesday, the headline of Jornal do Brasil is entitled "Forga da Verdade" (Forge of Truth) Part of the article follows:

> The government is worried about Brazil's image abroad. And it's right. It is uncomfortable, to say the least, to see Brazil appear abroad in an unflattering way, contradicting its traditions and cultural heritage. At a controversial time like the present, the negative image can have various causes and components. However, leaving aside the accessories, the recipe for improving the image is one: improve the country. Image is projected, it is a consequence. The government has an eloquent example at home. Just look at how the success of the economic and financial policy is reflected abroad. There is no intrigue, no fame, no bad faith that can destroy or deform an achievement that even newspapers that are not very sympathetic to the Revolution are already calling the **'Brazilian Miracle'**.[66]

The economic development celebrated by the newspaper was used as a way of overshadowing the negative image of the Medici government abroad. This negative image was initially linked to the genocide of indigenous people. In turn, the propaganda of the "Brazilian miracle" was a way of defending the government against accusations of violence. It is the economy, therefore, that carries the *"Force of Truth"*. In this conception, the violence practiced by the government does not deserve to be taken into account when economic policy is successful. Furthermore, a government that maintains a growing economic policy is committed to its nation and, therefore, other practices do not deserve to be questioned, because they do not carry the truth of the economy - they are nothing more than "intrigue" and "mischief". For this reason, commitment to economic policy would never allow the government's image to be tarnished by accusations of any kind, even if they were as serious as the genocide of traditional populations.

In addition to the indigenous genocide, other accusations contributed to the

---

66 Jornal do Brasil, 12/05/1970, 'A Forga da Verdade', p.1, emphasis added.

negative image of the Medici government abroad. The article continues:

Now, the government seems determined to sweep aside another heavy accusation - that of torture and violence against political prisoners. The libel against Brazil has been woven gradually and insistently. As in the case of radio, the national image has been distorted more or less everywhere. In large and respectable newspapers, we have been portrayed as a nation of torturers, indulging in the sadistic rage of an ideological fanaticism without law or king. The government is rightly concerned and is trying to improve its image. But a country's image can't be improved by correspondence, i.e. a letter, however well-written and well-intentioned, from ambassadors to media outlets that broadcast depressing news about Brazil isn't enough. The right way is to show the truth, no holds barred.[67]

Economics reappears as the path to truth. In the newspaper's view, defending the government against accusations of alleged torture would not be done with arguments contained in a "well-written and well-intentioned letter"[68] . The right way would be to "show the truth". At the time, Brazil's truth was the strength of its economy. At the time, the success of the Brazilian economy shielded the government from accusations of torture. In this sense, the economic development of the time was able to seduce Brazilians to the point where the abuses of the dictatorship remained alien to a large part of the population.

It is worth noting that the economic miracle appeared for the first time in Jornal do Brasil alongside denunciations of genocide and torture in Brazil in the 70s. Once again, the "golden years" and the "years of lead" appear side by side. The success of the economy justifies and authorizes the violence of the dictatorship. This means that the "Brazilian miracle" is also used to stifle abuses of power. As mentioned earlier, despite being supposedly antagonistic, the characterizations of the Medici government come closer when we look at some of the regime's legitimacy mechanisms. At the start of the third government, there was already evidence of the "years of lead", just as the appearance of the "Brazilian miracle" attested to the start of the dictatorship's golden years. Gold and lead appeared side by side in the national press.

But the discussion of the uses of what has come to be called the "Brazilian miracle" is not limited to the ability to manipulate economic indices. The moment of developmental euphoria was only possible when the daily lives of the population

---

67 Jornal do Brasil, 12/05/1970, 'A Forga da Verdade', p. 1.
68 On the government   's defense against accusations of torture, see: MONTENEGRO, 2012.

began to be altered by the increase in capitalist productivity. As the government stimulated the modernization of capitalism in the country, Brazilians were overwhelmed by the wave of national development.

The government's strategy for making the population feel the modernization of the capitalist system was to encourage work. The increase in job vacancies and the provision of jobs allowed the dictatorship to respond to the interests of the population. This strategy appears in one of the President's speeches[69] :

> Orderly work in the countryside, in factories and in commerce; the efforts of everyone to increase production and productivity; the enthusiasm and creativity of the business community, all of whom were confident in government action and in Brazil's future - all of this contributed decisively to the success of the economic and financial policy.[70]

The success of the economic and financial policy is then attributed to work in the countryside[71] and in the city. According to what the president says, in the enthusiasm for work, in *"everyone's effort* to increase productivity", there is confidence in government action. Once there is trust in the relationship between the government and the population, the way is open for state intervention. Order is established, opposition loses its strength. Of course, we can't measure popular support for the dictatorship by Medici's words. It would be too naïve to stick this discourse to historical experience. However, if the dictatorship remained in power for so many years, if it was able to commit a series of atrocities and still keep the generals in office, it is up to historiography to look at any and all mechanisms that contributed to the continuity of this government. The official speeches allow us to visualize the dictatorship's attempt to win the support of the population. I insist: the economy and, consequently, work, were avenues for government intervention; and the Brazilian miracle was an event that made people believe in the capacity and success of the dictatorship's government. Still using the "Brazilian miracle" as a backdrop, let's look

---

69 On December 31, 1972, in a speech entitled "The Brazilian Miracle", Medici addressed society on radio and television. It was a "happy new year" speech, extolling the achievements of 1972 and promising more for the following year. Given that the "Brazilian miracle" had already appeared in the press two years before this pronouncement, by this time this wording was more familiar to the population, making it easier for Medici to exploit it in his speeches.

70 MEDICI, EMILIO GARRASTAZU. **Tarefa de todos nos**. National Press Department, 2ª ed, 1973.

71 In the countryside, the Medici government's economic policy gave way "to large, mechanized agricultural units - increasing production and enabling the emergence of new crops, such as soya, the export champion, and citrus fruits (REIS FILHO, 2014)".

at another pronouncement that endorses the developmentalist euphoria in the country:

> The truth is, however, that there is no miracle behind this phenomenon.
> It does stem from the calm and balanced action of the government, from bold initiatives and courageous legal reforms; from the expansion of economic frontiers, from the occupation of huge empty spaces; from national and social integration; from the use of our potential wealth and the **valorization of our human resources**. Brazilian development also derives from the combination of private initiative and government action to open up foreign trade. It also stems from the mobilization of national savings, from stimulating investment, from correcting regional imbalances and, in particular, from the rational formulation of major programs in the fields of education, health, social assistance, communications, transport, basic industry and transformation. It also stems from the revision of working methods in agriculture, through the implementation of modern technology, the use of mechanization, fertilizers, selected seeds, the promotion of agro-industry, the construction of a wide network of processing plants, warehouses and silos. It also stems from the coherence of the **free enterprise economic system, compatible with the democratic form of government,** to increase productive work and productivity in all sectors, so that the **fruits of progress are distributed to all** regions and all Brazilians. The Brazilian miracle, in short, has a name and that name is - **work**.[72]

With these words, the president shifts the idea of a miracle to stimulating work. If at the beginning of the speech the general encourages the role of the nation in development, later on he replies that it is through work that his government intends to continue the modernization of the country. The miracle, once a divine accomplishment, loses its supernatural character to be endowed with humanity. The miracle is work, the result of human will and practice. According to the official discourse, the causes of the "miracle" lie in the government's commitment and will, and the merits of economic policy lie in its confidence and faith in its work.

The same pronouncement describes some of the government's main development efforts; I have highlighted some of these tasks. Starting with the "expansion of economic frontiers, the occupation of immense empty spaces; national and social integration; the use of our potential wealth and the valorization of our human resources". The strategy consisted of increasing national productivity through a program of integrating non-industrialized regions. To carry out this program, the dictatorship redirected the surplus workforce to the "immense empty spaces". In these new workplaces were the "potential riches" that had not yet been exploited, where the government encouraged private enterprise to create "economic frontiers" that would

---

72 MEDICI, 1973, p. 16/17, emphasis added.

absorb the migrant labor force. These projects were the basis of the National Integration Program. The empty spaces refer to the Amazon, a region where Brazil's riches have yet to be systematically exploited. In turn, the policies for "valuing human resources" favored workers from the Northeast, a region with a large population, a lot of poverty and little employment. Once relocated to the Amazon, these workers would be absorbed by the work fronts built in partnership with the private sector in that region. To receive them in these new locations, settlement programs were planned on the banks of the highways to be built in the region.

Amazonia.

The state is looking for a way to stimulate, determine and guide people's activities so that they are effectively useful to it. This calculation involves the number of individuals it intends to govern, the needs of these people so that they can live, and the healthy condition in which they can occupy themselves, work and carry out their activities. Avoid idleness; put all those who can work to work.[73]

Therefore, the "Brazilian miracle", beyond the growth of economic indices, can only be guaranteed at the cost of the controlled insertion of bodies into the productive apparatus and through the adjustment of population phenomena to economic processes. *The Brazilian miracle is work,* and requires the participation and engagement of the population in government projects aimed at increasing productivity in the country:

> In this sense, it is necessary to understand the Milagre in a broader sense, as a way of being in the world at that time which, in addition to the possibilities of economic ascension, also offered a certain vision of the past and expectations of a promising future, based on a present in which these people should only live according to established social norms. In other words, the Miracle offered significant sections of society an idea according to which work and obedience to the norms and institutions of the present meant respect for the Fatherland, its history and the great men of the nation, and at the same time, the construction of a prosperous future[74].

The quote is fundamental for broadening our view of work. The historian's words contribute to the analysis of the shift made in the words of Medici himself: the miracle is work to the extent that we understand it as a given way of being in the

---

73 FOUCAULT, 2008.
74 CORDERO, 2012, p. 99.

world. In other words, as well as enabling economic growth, the developmentalist euphoria spread the expectation that, at the beginning of the 1970s, Brazil was building the foundations for a modern future. Economic policy was charged with expectation, as well as offering a positive view of the political experience of the dictatorship. The coup of 1964 set the country on the road to progress. The population, for its part, could not be exempt from this process. It was up to people to take their places in production to contribute to the country of the future, as well as turning a blind eye to the institutional violence committed only against those who hindered this process.

2.4.2 The *years of lead*

Today it is common to look back at the 1970s and realize that Medici went down in history as "the man under whose presidency Brazil would witness the height of the repression unleashed by the military dictatorship"[75] . His political career in the Brazilian Army, the violence that marked the years of his mandate and some of the general's polemical statements during and after the dictatorship, made Garrastazu Medici a symbol of military repression in the years of the dictatorship.

In April 1964, at the time of the military coup, Medici was then commander of the Agulhas Negras Military Academy and was at the disposal of the movement that ousted then president Joao Goulart. But it was during the Costa e Silva administration, the second government of the dictatorship, that Medici rose to prominence in public office. In 1967, he became head of the SNI (National Intelligence Service), an intelligence organization created by the regime. When it was created, the SNI was responsible for setting up a comprehensive information network to help the government make its decisions. Under Medici, "more than an advisory and informative body, the SNI became an advisory body, capable of vetoing names

---

75 FICO, Carlos. *Alem do Golpe - Verses and controversies about 1964 and the Military Dictatorship.* Sao Paulo: Record, 2004, p. 77.

considered for public positions[76] " As head of the SNI, Medici took part in the presidential meeting that instituted AI-5 (Institutional Act Number Five)[77] . His statement at that meeting, which was later made public, shows Medici's unconditional support for the dictatorship's most authoritarian decree:

> Mr. President, ladies and gentlemen. I feel perfectly at ease (...) and, why not say it, very satisfied, in giving my approval to the document that has been presented to me. This is because, Mr. President, at a meeting of the National Security Council, in the performance of the duties assigned to me by Your Excellency, as head of the SNI, I had the opportunity to give a detailed account of the Brazilian national situation and to demonstrate to the councilors that, in fact and in action, what was on the streets was counter-revolution. I believe, Mr. President, that with your democratic background, you were too tolerant, because on that occasion I was already asking (...) that exceptional measures be taken to combat the counter-revolution that was on the streets. That's all I had to say[78] .

The document Medici refers to is precisely AI-5; the "counter-revolution" was the growing resistance to the dictatorship during 1968[79] . Medici's stance during the meeting was a sign of the regime's authoritarian policy. If it had been up to the then head of the SNI, exceptional measures of this nature would have been requested sooner. The promulgation of AI-5 was a *turning point* in the dictatorship. From the release of this Institutional Act to the amnesty law[80] violent repression was a constant in the regime. AI-5 dissolved Congress and established the legal mechanisms to institutionalize, even more effectively, police and military repression of individuals, institutions and movements that in various ways resisted the dictatorship. Promulgated on December 13, 1968, AI-5 was only extinguished ten years later, on October 13, 1978. The years during which this decree was in force comprised the entire term of

---

[76] FICO, 2004, p. 77.

[77] "A kind of *decretum terrible* that made the regime, which until then had respected some basic rights, definitively authoritarian. From the Act onwards, torture became a systematic practice after arrests and during interrogations of all those suspected of subversion" (FICO, 2012, p. 68).

78 GASPARI, 2002, p. 132.

79 The 100,000 march was what became known as a large popular demonstration of resistance to the dictatorship. It took place in Rio de Janeiro on June 26, 1968 to denounce the arbitrary actions of the dictatorship. An   important account of this event can be found in the book "1968, the year that didn't end", by Zuenir Ventura (VENTURA, Zuenir. 1968 - the year that didn't end. Editora Nova Fronteira. Rio de Janeiro, 1988).

80 Law No. 6.683, of August 28, 1979. Promulgated by General-President Figueiredo, the law granted amnesty for political and electoral crimes in the period between September 2, 1961 and August 15, 1979. The amnesty was granted to both the crimes of the left and the crimes of the dictatorship, thereby clearing the military and torturers who actively participated in the repression.

General Garrastazu Medici. Having been responsible for almost half of the years that saw the execution of AI-5 was decisive for the subsequent definition of Medici as a hard-line general and of his government as part of the dictatorship's years of lead.

Therefore, guided by the AI-5, the Medici government was responsible for the years in which the dictatorship hardened its repression. But for repression to exist, it had to be accompanied by resistance to the regime. At this point, another question arises. The operation that defines the period as part of the so-called "years of lead" is linked not only to the violence of the government, but to the war that the armed forces established with the organizations of armed resistance to the dictatorship - the guerrillas.

The Araguaia Guerrilla was a major undertaking of the militant left during the years of the dictatorship. Linked to the rural side of the guerrilla movement, this event represented

> A Marxist-inspired armed uprising that aimed to unleash a revolutionary people's war in Brazil, starting in the countryside and conquering the cities. The Communist Party of Brazil promoted the movement in the region of the Araguaia River at the confluence of four states, an area known as Bico do Papagaio. The fighting took place inside the Amazon rainforest, in a polygon of approximately 6,500 square kilometers between Para and Goias (now Tocantins), an area slightly larger than the Federal District, where around 20,000 people lived[81] .

The guerrilla war lasted from 1967 to 1974. In other words, it lasted all the years of the Medici government. It was during this general's mandate that the guerrillas were practically annihilated. In the first months of 1974, before the general had left office, the military had already begun to leave the region. On the other hand, if we consider the death of the last member of the resistance as the final mark of the guerrilla war, we will have to attribute the defeat of the guerrillas to the subsequent government, of which General Ernesto Geisel was president. But "when he took over the presidency in March 1974, Ernesto Geisel would have corroborated everything he found armed - including the torture and summary executions"[82] . The order to eliminate the guerrilla members came from a negotiation between President Medici and his army minister, Orlando Geisel, the brother of the next president, Ernesto

---

81 STUDART, Hugo. *The law of the jungle,* Sao Paulo: Geragao Editorial, 2006, p. 16.
82 STUDART, Hugo. *The law of the jungle,* Sao Paulo: Geragao Editorial, 2006, p. 272.

Geisel.

In yet another compromising statement, this time in an interview with Veja magazine, Medici confessed to giving the order to assassinate the guerrillas:

> Once, the military ministers wanted to use the armed forces to fight terrorism, but I wouldn't let them: "That's a job for the police," I told them. But there was a firefight in a unit and a major died while rescuing a sergeant who had been wounded. So I had a conversation with the Minister of the Army, Orlando Geisel, and asked: 'But do only our people die? When they invade a device, they'll have to invade with machine gun fire. We're at war and we can't sacrifice our own people. There's no doubt that it was a war, after which it was possible to restore peace to Brazil. I put an end to terrorism in this country[83] .

The above account is yet another trace that allows us to associate General Medici with the hard-line profile of the Army, as well as situating his government in the so-called "years of lead" of the dictatorship. According to Garrastazu Medici, the dictatorship's violence was the result of a war waged against "terrorism". In Medici's view, terrorism was identified in the armed actions of the organizations resisting the regime. The military's repression and violence was then justified as a form of defense against terrorism. In general, the guerrilla organizations wanted to stimulate a popular war that would lead the country to a socialist revolution. In the view of these armed groups, the dictatorship represented a government of exception committed to the capitalist project. The military's participation in this regime was a manoeuvre by the bourgeoisie to block the advance of Marxist-inspired political mobilization[84] .

The fact is that the concept of the left did not spread among the working class. Criticism of the dictatorship did not resonate with the working class and the proposal for revolution was never understood by the poorest sections of Brazilian society. At the beginning of the 1970s, the repression took advantage of the country's economic well-being to crush left-wing groups without any repercussions for the government's image. Enveloped by the euphoria of development, the majority of the Brazilian population seemed blind to the atrocities of the regime. Historian Daniel Araao Reis, a member of one of the left-wing groups that took part in the urban guerrilla war, says

---

83 Emilio Garrastazu Medici, statement to the FGV CPDoc. In Veja Magazine, Sao Paulo, October 1998, p. 74.
    In STUDART, 2006, p. 270.
84 DREIFUSS, 1981.

that "that war, as the left-wing militants and the political police called it, was something that the majority of the population couldn't understand, let alone participate in directly[85] ". In an attempt to understand the behavior of society in the face of the acts of resistance, the historian continues:

> Contrary to what those involved in the actions imagined, few shared their convictions and certainties. And these were indispensable for taking the risks and going through the sacrifices inherent in the challenge posed by the dictatorship. On the other hand, it's not certain that there was sympathy for the brutal methods used by the torturers, although a large part of Brazilian society had already learned to live with torture serenely, if it was only used against so-called marginals. As long as the dirty game took place out of sight and out of earshot, in filthy, stinking, soundproof cells, it was always possible to maintain that the excesses were ignored and society was innocent. And that's what many people do to this day[86] .

Despite the difficulty in making the war against the dictatorship massive, the lack of understanding of the left's project, "ignorance" and "innocence" are arguments that justify the passivity of a large part of the population in the face of abuses committed by authoritarian governments. And "that's what many people do to this day", perpetuating a logic that naturalizes oppression of all kinds.

Years later, at the beginning of the 1980s, when signs of a democratic transition began to appear, the abuses of the dictatorship in Brazil also began to be recognized by Brazilian institutions. As far as the Medici government was concerned, as the democratic transformation progressed "the memory of the years of lead prevailed over that of the golden years"[87] . The redemocratization movement consolidated a memory of the dictatorship marked by the memory of the violence of that period. However, the campaign to denounce the torture and murders committed by the Brazilian state during the regime kept society in the position of victim of the military's violence. In the political movement that led to the democratic transition, it was customary to blame only the military for the repression, hiding the participation of civilian leaders in the dictatorship government itself. In other words, the discourses that "blamed" the military found a place in the process of re-democratization to the extent that they also exonerated the regime's civilian leaders. The civilian leaders who took part in the

---

[85]   REIS, 2014, p. 78.

86 REIS FILHO, 2014, p. 78.

[87]   CORDEIRO, 2014, p. 194.

dictatorship's government led the democratic transition and continued as politicians in the new regime:

> And let the record show that the "milicos" left the government without being stoned - just as they had entered it without having to fire a shot. However, the obsession with characterizing the dictatorship solely as military led, and still leads today, many to mark 1985 as the year that marked the end of the regime, because it was there that the last general-president's mandate ended. The irony is that he was succeeded by a politician - Jose Sarney - who had supported the dictatorship from the outset, becoming, over time, one of its main leaders... civilians[88] .

While agreeing with the thesis that the movement for re-democratization consolidated the memory of the years of lead, we also agree that this memory responds to a historical construction in which some politicians from the dictatorship participated. In this construction, there would be no lead if there were no resistance. The violence of the dictatorship years is linked not only to the authoritarianism of the military, but also to the revolutionary resistance of the period. Thus, the magic power to name the political events of the dictatorship remained in the hands of hegemonic groups who, while legitimizing their place in the political transition, disqualified the revolutionary events of yesteryear. "This is called hegemony, when the victors manage to make the vanquished use their vocabulary, carrying pejorative connotations"[89] . The naming of periods transcends the work of the historian, while allowing for the investigation of the nuances of a complex historical process, such as the Brazilian military dictatorship between the 1960s and 1980s. Therefore, *to* call the Medici government the "years of lead" is to use a denomination given by the victors.

The consolidation of democracy in Brazil took place during a historical period in which the actions of revolutionary groups no longer found a place in society. The socialist dream was crumbling along with the Soviet Union. If there were no longer any threats to the capitalist order, there was no longer any need to defend the national order and, therefore, the presence of the military in government lost its meaning. The time had come for the population to choose their presidents. Democracy was taking hold in a political climate where there was no room for military dictatorship or revolutionary organizations.

---

88 REIS FILHO, 2012.
89 REIS FILHO, 2014, p. 75

The 1964 coup, the years of dictatorship and the process of re-democratization are national historical experiences marked by the polarized conflict between socialism and capitalism. The capitalism/communism duality is a way of being in the world not only during the first years of the 1970s, but throughout the political experience of the dictatorship. In this sense,

> The world that fell apart in the 1980s was the world formed by the impact of the Russian Revolution of 1917. We were all marked by it, to the extent that we got used to thinking of the modern industrial economy in terms of binary opposites, capitalism and socialism, as mutually exclusive alternatives[90].

During the 1980s, the collapse of the Soviet Union put an end to the bipolar world between capitalism and socialism. In the same process, at the same time, the dictatorship in Brazil was making its transition to democracy. With the fall of the socialist world, the justifications for the dictatorship also fell, as there was no longer any need for an "exception" government to safeguard the country from foreign, communist, Soviet and/or Marxist threats. It was in the 1980s, when bipolarity broke down, that the dictatorship made its transition. The Democratic Rule of Law was reborn as a kind of third way between the dictatorship's government and the socialist project of the organizations resisting the regime.

Before taking up the narrative of the Medici government's policies, we must not lose sight of the fact that the new challenges posed to the historiography of the period are in response to the attempt to establish questions about the social bases, adherence and political functioning of the dictatorship. In order to write this history, it is necessary to put aside the denominations of the period as "years of lead" or "golden years", as well as the definition of Medici as a "hard-line" general:

> From the perspective of historiography, it is possible to see a strong tendency to define what leaders, public men or even simple people have been or are, establishing fixed identities instead of thinking of them in their multiple and diverse relationships, discourses and actions. In this respect, the fixed identity is projected as transhistorical or even ahistorical[91].

Classifications and identity attributions are dangerous because they imprison, reduce and crystallize historical views. In the course of these lines, the specificity of

---

90 HOBSBAWN, 2001 *apud* STUDART, 2006, p. 185.
91 MONTENEGRO, 2012, p. 24.

the discussion around the Medici government does not involve trying to pin down this or that key word. The insistence on defining a certain period as the "years of lead", or the profile of the generals as "hardliners", has created generalizing notions about the dictatorship. That's why I've chosen to outline some criticisms of the regime's social memory. By removing old adjectives, I aim to build new horizons for understanding the Medici government. It is these new interpretative schemes that make it possible to articulate other dialogues and other criticisms, thus establishing new approaches to the present time.

2.5 "Integrating for development" - territory, economy and politics

The insistence on development was a hallmark of the Medici government. The historical uniqueness of this task is linked to the effort to integrate the different regions of the national territory economically. In the first half of the 1970s, development policies were accompanied by a series of articulated objectives. These objectives allow us to better visualize the political experience of that historical moment.

The book *Metas e Bases para Agao de Governo* (1970)[92] contains some of the Medici government's planning studies. At the time of its publication, the dictatorship had already appointed its third president - which meant the regime had to deal with the legacies of previous administrations. In the official rhetoric, the dictatorship's project continued, but the Medici government had to carry out a program that was specific to it. In other words, its guidelines mix originality, influences from previous administrations, and projects aimed at continuing the dictatorship's government program. Let's see:

> Consolidating the basic achievements of the First and Second Governments of the Revolution, the Third Government will take an important step towards eliminating the gap between the country's physical assets and its economic size; and in this way, during its term, it will **propel Brazil towards the fullness of accelerated** and self-

---

92 MINISTRY OF PLANNING, 1970.

<blockquote>
sustaining **development, while** effectively leading it to relative job stability **in a climate of security and social and political stability**. In the latter area, a realistic effort will be made to progressively evolve towards building a politically open society, which reconciles the need to accelerate development with the maintenance of freedoms and with the greatest possible degree of participation by private initiative and the decentralization of economic activity[93] .
</blockquote>

Right from the start, the challenge that the "Third Government" would have to face was "to eliminate the gap between the country's physical assets and its economic size". This would be a fundamental step towards putting Brazil on the road to full development. The assets, goods and wealth available for capitalist exploitation were incompatible with the economic stage the country was at. Brazil had sufficient resources available for development. In this sense, government intervention was needed to take advantage of the riches on a national scale, in order to modernize the economy and achieve "the fullness of accelerated development". This mission was reserved for the Medici government. For this government, the development of the economy presupposed the economic articulation of the national territory. Only by taking advantage of the physical patrimony, given by the borders limiting the intervention of the Brazilian state, would the country achieve the longed-for economic modernization. The objective of development is to integrate the territory into the modern capitalist exploitation regime.

But development also appeared to be linked to the problem of national security, since it could only be achieved in a climate of "social and political stability". Just as development required the exploitation of the country's physical heritage, security involved concern for the national territory. With the territory as its horizon, the government would achieve development and guarantee national security: it would hit two birds with one stone. The use of unexploited natural wealth could only be carried out in conjunction with the defense of these assets from international covetousness.

This conception was greatly stimulated by the dictatorship's declared intention to keep the social order protected from "terrorist" and/or "anti-democratic" threats, in other words, protected from the threats of communist countries. As an official document attests, "the 1970s (...) will see the exacerbation of social and political

---

93 MINISTERIO DO PLANEJAMENTO, 1970, p. 6, emphasis added.

tensions"[94] . The beginning of the 1970s represented the intensification of the so-called Cold War on the world stage. At that time, international politics was divided between the socialist countries, led by the USSR, and the "capitalist West", the territory of influence of the United States (US). The socialist countries were notably led by closed political regimes - with a single party in government - and an economy of strict state control. Capitalist countries, on the other hand, generally represented bourgeois democracy and a free market economy, with low taxes and periodic elections.

Having exposed the polarity that marked international politics, the task now is to understand the role that Brazil played in this dispute. A series of practices sometimes brought this or that country closer and sometimes distanced it from this or that influence. Despite this, the Medici government was aware of the dispute and the tendency with which it wanted to associate itself. In general, Brazil, like other South American countries, was going through dictatorial political regimes, which were extremely authoritarian and police-like, at the same time as their economies were directed in the North American capitalist direction - free enterprise.

According to the Ministry of Planning, the Medici government would reconcile "the need to accelerate development with the maintenance of freedoms and the greatest possible degree of participation by private initiative"[95] . Therefore, in order to develop the economy or to boost capitalism in the country, making it more competitive and modern, the government relied on the participation of private initiative. This alliance allows us to see an important segment in the formation of the dictatorship's government. From what the document presents, it also seems to me that "the civilian dimension of the dictatorial regime is unquestionable, even if the top of the pyramid of power was occupied by the military leaders (AARAO REIS, 2014).

So far, the Medici government's concern with economic policy has been presented in the context of its planning. Before we go into the merits of implementing integration policies, I would like to point out the areas where interventions were forged for the global task of development:

---

[94] MINISTRY OF PLANNING, 1970, p.6
[95] MINISTRY OF PLANNING, 1970, p.6

In the 1970s, this global task had to be embodied in a National Development Project, in which the people could not be mere spectators but the main protagonists, with a view to implementing a national action plan to 'coordinate, integrate and catalyze our efforts'. The project is based on the political decision to promote development through work and intelligence, building a future for the whole nation capable of breaking with the dimensions of the past[96].

The idea that in the seventies we were living in a future capable of breaking with the dimensions of the past points to the Medici government as a decisive gesture for the country's direction. The rumor of progress was part of the developmentalist euphoria of those years. But note that the National Development Project is presented as a goal that the government is not capable of achieving on its own. The success of economic policy would depend on the protagonism of the people, in other words, popular participation in the realization of government practices. The achievement of high economic indices would only be possible when the population became part of this program. Once society took responsibility, took it upon itself, embodied the government's achievements and programs, it declared its adherence to the Brazilian state's project in the early 1970s.

In the Ministry of Planning's text, some passages refer back to old considerations and others point to new discussions. Firstly, the role of the people in the Development Project reinforces government policies as being centered on the population. There can be no government without the control and agency of the people for whom it is responsible. There is no government if there are no governed; even if these positions are not restricted between those who occupy the state and those who are oppressed by it.

But what is new in this section is the perspective of development action as a coordinated and integrated effort. We already know that the Medici government's economic orientation followed a developmentalist policy. However, it is the insistence on integrated development that makes the experience put into practice by the third government of the dictatorship unique. Articulating its potential and minimizing the "social problems around the country", the government put into practice what it believed to be a reorganization of Brazil's economic structure. Based on the conception that national destiny was indivisible, the government was convinced that

---

96 MINISTRY OF PLANNING, 1970, p. 15.

the process of modernizing the country's economy involved integrating the peripheral regions into the national productivity regime. Development would be the result of a policy that integrated the regions of Brazil and took advantage of their "natural riches." Productive forces, markets, labor and investments are articulated according to the notions that government rationality has of each region of the national territory. From this perspective, the Northeast was the place for labor; the Amazon, the place for agricultural production, the saddler of the world; and in the Center-South, the developed core, were industry and the initial investments for economic growth.

In a nutshell, then, we can conclude that the strategy for development and the achievement of the government's primary objectives is to incorporate new areas into the country's total economy and, at the same time, to make better use of the population as a resource, an abundant labor force. These were also the terms in which the National Integration Program was carried out.

One of the aims of studying the National Integration Program is to show how development policies are geared towards absorbing poor regions and populations into the modern regime of capitalist exploitation. In the NIP, territory is a key dimension of its policies. In other works, I have been able to untangle the threads of national integration and point out how national security policies go hand in hand with development policies. Occupying the borders and protecting the country from foreign threats, relocating populations of rural workers to avoid conflicts over land and the consequent use of these conflicts by the national left. Within these policies, it is possible to discuss the problem of legitimacy and social adherence to the regime at the time of its third government. Finally, another way forward is to show how state policies are population policies, conceived by controlling individuals as a set of people to be governed.

The perspective that marks out my varied studies on National Integration goes hand in hand with some guiding questions: what should the state be concerned with? How did the Medici government deal with the desires, interests and needs of the Brazilian population in the early 1970s? Rather than proposing conclusions, my work as a whole aims to raise questions about the period under study. The first half of the

1970s is a projection of time that is difficult to rationalize, but which can be understood if we investigate the government techniques used by the Brazilian state during that period.

3. THE ACTUALITY OF THE DICTATORSHIP AND THE HISTORY WE HAVE LIVED THROUGH[97]

Despite accelerated economic growth in the 1970s, Brazil is still regarded as the country of the future[98] . We still live with the promises of an economic power that has never been realized. Similar to the dictatorship, the public policies of the current democracy are still committed to capitalist development. The condition of emerging country remains in Brazil's classification in relation to the world economy. Many heads of government, even after the years of civil-military dictatorship, continue to promise to put Brazil on the level of the industrialized countries[99] .

The "third government of the revolution" believed that economic development could only be achieved with the greatest possible degree of participation by the private sector and the decentralization of economic activity. *In the* same vein, after the re-establishment of democracy, the Fernando Henrique Cardoso government (1994-2002) opened up the alliance between the public authorities and the business community, privatizing a series of services and basic industries. Subsequently, the Workers' Party government (2002-2015) maintained the alliance with large private enterprises, such as the FIFA World Cup[100] . Another characteristic that brings the current government closer to the practices of the dictatorship is the transformation of the country into a construction site, where pharaonic projects have gained prominence in the set of government policies - such as the construction of the Belo Monte hydroelectric dam.

In the study of government rationality, comparison is inevitable. Subject to the specificities of each era, constructions such as the Transamazonica highway and the

---

97 FICO, Carlos. Historia que temos vivido *in* VARELLA, F. F.; MOLLO, H. M; PEREIRA, M. H. F.; MATA, S. (eds.) Tempo presente e usos do passado. Rio de Janeiro: Editora FGV, 2012.
98 At the time, the growth in economic indicators was impressive and, according to ARAAO REIS, *"it is impressive to this day, since the country has never shown such high results: 9.5% in 1970; 11.3 in 1971; 10.4% in 1972; 11.4% in 1973 (AARAO REIS, 2014, p. 79)"*
99 Today, Brazil is a member of a political and economic cooperation group that brings together some countries considered to be emerging markets. The group is called BRICS and is made up of the initials of the member countries: Brazil, Russia, India and *South* Africa.
100 Federation *Internationale de Football Association (FIFA)*. FIFA is the organizer of the Football World Cup, today's leading sporting event. The organization brings together 209 member countries and territories.

Rio-Niteroi bridge were presented as "showcases of a modern Brazil"[101] . In democracy, the "mega" projects of the FIFA World Cup and the Belo Monte hydroelectric plant were carried out under promises of development. Worse than being guided by developmentalist guidelines, the implementation of major government projects continues without measuring the consequences of their social impacts. Note that among the pharaonic works of the dictatorship and democracy are two interventions in the Brazilian Amazon. In the 1970s, the Transamazonica. Today, Belo Monte. A specialist in studies of the region, Viveiros de Castro[102] compares the development ambiguity of the democratic governments to what he calls the megalomania of progress during the dictatorship. According to him, just like during the dictatorship, the current road projects and the construction of hydroelectric plants in the Amazon, together with the benefits for agribusiness, represent a disregard for the rights of indigenous peoples. For the anthropologist, when it comes to the Amazon, the military regime *(on the right) is* closer to the political project of the Workers' Party *(on the left)* during the years of its government. What makes this comparison possible is precisely the insistence on capitalist development:

> It took the left, a former guerrilla, to carry out the right's project. In fact, they always wanted the same thing, which was to rule over the people. The right and the left thought they knew what was best for the people and, what's worse, what they thought was best was very similar. The military may have been more violent, more fascist, but the fact is that it's very similar. (...) [the left in general] has a congenital inability to think about all kinds of people other than the good worker who is going to become a consumer. An enormous inability to understand the populations that have refused to play the game of capitalism. Those who haven't entered the game - the Indians, the rubber tappers, the peasants, the quilombolas - people who want to live in peace, who want to keep to themselves, they don't understand. (...) [the left] has this conception of production, that living and producing - 'work is the essence of man'101

To criticize recent government policies in the Amazon, Viveiros de Castro compares President Dilma's government with the dictatorship. In this statement, the intellectual mobilizes the past to strengthen his arguments. As he draws on the dictatorship, he historicizes Dilma's government and problematizes her intentions. By making the past present, it was possible to demonstrate that some of Brazil's current

---

[101] LAMB, 2012.

102 Eduardo Viveiros de Castro is a Brazilian anthropologist and professor at the National Museum of the Federal University of Rio de Janeiro.

policies are heading in the same direction as those chosen by the military who occupied the presidency of the republic.

The political uses of historical experiences contribute directly to reflections on the present. Using the comparison made by Viveiros de Castro and with reference to the studies of Hartog & Revel (2002), I understand that "the contemporary debate on the past has surpassed the historian's capacity to direct it"[103104] . But anthropologists, and intellectuals in general, are not the only ones capable of sharing with historians the ability to direct the contemporary debate on the past. Other subjects, linked from different places of enunciation, also make political use of the past. In Brazil, it is even possible to find other parallels between the government of democracy and the government of General Garrastazu Medici. Let's take a look:

Figure 1 | The Cup of all Cups - Latuff, 2014. Taken from <latuffcartoonswordpress.com>.

Carlos Henrique de Sousa, known as Latuff, is not a historian, but he uses the past to construct a political reflection on the present. The cartoon depicts, from right to left, the then governor of the state of São Paulo, Geraldo Alckmin, President Dilma

---

102Interview conducted by Rafael Cariello for Revista Piauí, issue 88, year 8, January 2014, p. 18.
103 KNAUSS, Paulo. Uses of the past and history of the present: archives of repression and historical knowledge. In VARELLA, F. F.; MOLLO, H. M; PEREIRA, M. H. F.; MATA, S. (eds.). Present time and uses of the past. Rio de Janeiro: Editora FGV, 2012, p. 152.

Roussef and President Medici's "esplrito" (this one next to his tombstone, which in turn indicates the year of birth and death of the late general) 103. The suggestion is clear: Medici is dead, he belongs to the past, he belongs to history. Alckmin and Dilma, alive, beg for inspiration from the former president: "O master! inspire us to make the cup of cups!" - cries Dilma. The president's plea was ratified by Geraldo Alckmin: "Amem!". Between June and July 2014, Brazil hosted the FIFA World Cup. This private venture relied on a firm partnership between businesspeople and the government. The expression *"cup of cups",* used in the cartoon, was uttered by the president in one of her speeches before the event104. Claiming that Brazil would host the "Cup of Cups" was tantamount to saying that Brazil would host the best competition so far. But why does Latuff use Medici? What effect did the cartoonist want to have? What policies of the dictatorship could inspire the democratic government to hold the World Cup?

We cannot underestimate the importance of the "economic miracle" of the Medici government. The government's development policies were decisive in building its legitimacy. The economic growth of the early 1970s was accompanied by torture, imprisonment, censorship, etc. The dictatorship paid the bill for the repression with the euphoria of development. At the time, there was a clear belief that the country was on a path of progress to become a national power. This political laboratory housed the dictatorship's formula: development and national security. The intention, therefore, was to boost capitalism in the country and crush any threat to this economic project.

But to what extent could Medici's *know-how* inspire Dilma and Geraldo Alckmin? Despite being a private event, the government had to pay out exorbitant amounts of public money for the World Cup to be held in Brazil. And to justify opening up the coffers, the World Cup was presented as a set of measures aimed at modernizing the country's economy. The main justification for spending public money on a private event was the promise that the World Cup would provide an important legacy for Brazil's development. Tourism would create jobs and the work required by FIFA, such as improving urban mobility and building the stadiums, would leave important legacies for the quality of life of the Brazilian population. Given that the FIFA World Cup was heavily invested in by the public authorities, it was a chance for politicians to boost the economy.

and attest to the success of the government's undertaking. Just like the *golden years,* the World *Cup years* produced a developmental euphoria similar to that of the 1970s.

Another issue brings the two political moments in the cartoon closer together: repression. From June 2013 until just before the World Cup final, street demonstrations broke out across the country. The common denominator of the motivations that brought people to the streets was the questioning of the government's efforts to organize the World Cup and the trigger, at least in the capitals, was the increase in public transport fares[105] . While spending millions on the event, the government failed to address the precarious structure of its basic public services. In order not to lose the thread of the discussion, it is important to state that a large part of the World Cup works were linked to the progressive illusion of "a nation that dreams of being a 'power', but which cannot overcome basic problems"[106] .

Faced with the growth of the movements that took to the streets of the big cities, the government, in order to safeguard the enterprise that had become the World Cup, in other words, to safeguard the orientation of its developmentalist economic policy, had to put in place a whole apparatus of repression against the demonstrations. As the demonstrations grew, FIFA threatened to cancel the event in Brazil. In the years of the dictatorship, even with deliberate repression, General Medici's government was able to keep the torture under wraps so as not to jeopardize his image while he was President of the Republic. In recent years, the repression used by both the federal government and the government of Sao Paulo has relied on a police apparatus that has spared no effort in demobilizing demonstrations around the country. Just like Medici, today's politicians didn't want to see their development projects threatened. Violence, torture, arbitrary arrests, monitoring and persecution

---

104MARICATO, Emilia [et al]. Rebel Cities: Passe Livre and the demonstrations that took to the streets of Brazil. Sao Paulo: Boitempo : Carta Maior, 2013.
106 " (CORDEIRO, 2014, p. 201).

have been reported. Censorship of the press was also frequent, as it came from within the newsrooms themselves - the media entrepreneurs were surrendered to the economic policy of which the World Cup was the flagship.

Medici's inspiration for democratic politicians comes from his ability to combine confidence in development with a guarantee of security for public-private ventures. Development and national security also appear side by side in democracy. In other words, in the shadow of progress it was possible to hide the ruins of an authoritarian state. This was a hallmark of the civil-military dictatorship, especially during the years of General Garrastazu Medici's rule. Today's democracy works in a similar way. Still in the wake of development, its public actions are planned and put into practice without measuring the social consequences of the undertakings. Or rather, they do, but the problem is that their balance tends to tip in favor of the interests of certain political and business groups. In other words, the state goes to great lengths to defend the economic interests of the political and business elite.

On the other hand, political resistance and questioning of current government measures have been met with violence and repression. When using comparisons, there is no point in pointing to the dictatorship as the only repressive monster in Brazilian political history, when today we feel the police abuses of the democratic rule of law. Both dictatorships and democracies legitimize their forms of government by promising development, while crushing any questioning of their policies with police force. However, regardless of the level, it is not that repression and abuse went unnoticed, whether under dictatorship or democracy. It's just that, mobilized by other interests, part of the population prefers to be blind to the arbitrary actions of their government, whether under the dictatorship or the current democratic rule of law.

4. BIBLIOGRAPHICAL REFERENCES

AGAMBEN, Giorgio. *State of exception.* Sao Paulo: Boitempo Editorial, 2004.

AGOSTINHO, Gilberto. *Soccer and the Military Dictatorship in Brazil.* Nossa Historia Magazine, no. 14, December 2004

ARAUJO, Maria Paula Nascimento. *Fragmented Utopia: the new left in Brazil and the world in the 1970s.* FGV Editora, 2000

BARRETO, Tulio & FERREIRA, Laurindo (eds). *On the trail of the coup: 1964 revisited.* Recife: A fundagao; Editora Massangana, 2012

CORDEIRO, Janaina Martins. *Milagre, comemoraqdes e consenso ditatorial no Brasil,* 1972. *in* Confluenze Vol. 4, No. 2, 2012, pp. 82-102, ISSN 2036-0967, Dipartimento di Lingue, Letterature e Culture Moderne, Universita di Bologna.

CORDEIRO, Janaina. *Why remember? The collective memory of the Medici government and the dictatorship in Bage. In* REIS, Daniel Aarao; RIDENTI, Marcelo; MOTTA, Rodrigo Patto Sa

CORDEIRO, Janaina. *The dictatorship in times of miracle: celebrations, pride and consent.* Rio de Janeiro: Editora FGV, 2015.

DREIFUSS, Rene. Armand. *1964: the conquest of the State.* Petropolis: Vozes, 1981.

FICO, CARLOS. *"Espionage, political police, censorship and propaganda: the basic pillars of repression".* In Republican Brazil. The time of the dictatorship. The military regime and social movements at the end of the 20th century. Vol. 4. Rio de Janeiro: Civilizagao Brasileira, 2003.

FICO, Carlos. *Alem do Golpe - Verses and controversies about 1964 and the Military Dictatorship.* Sao Paulo: Record, 2004.

FOUCAULT, MICHEL. *What is an author? In Ditos e escritos vol. III Estetica: Literatura e Pintura, MUsica e Cinema.* Rio de Janeiro: Editora Forense Universitaria, 2001.

FOUCAULT, Michel. *The Order of Discourse.* Edigoes Loyola, 2009.

FOUCAULT, Michel. *Security, Territory and Population.* Sao Paulo: Martins Fontes, 2008.

FOUCAULT, Michel. *Microphysics of Power.* Organized and translated by Roberto

Machado. Rio de Janeiro: Edigoes Graal, 1984.

GASPARI, Helio. *A ditadura Escancarada vol. 2 - As ilusdes Armadas.* Sao Paulo: Compainha das Letras, 2012.

GINZBURG, Carlo. *Distance and perspective: two metaphors. In Wooden eyes: nine reflections on distance.* São Paulo: Companhia das Letras, 2001.

GUIMARAES NETO, Regina B. The *legend of the green gold: politics and colonization in contemporary Brazil.* Cuiaba: UNICEM, 2002.

KNAUSS, Paulo. *Uses of the past and history of the present: archives of repression and historical knowledge. In VARELLA, F. F.; MOLLO, H. M; PEREIRA, M. H. F.; MATA, S. (eds.). Present time and uses of the past.* Rio de Janeiro: Editora FGV, 2012.

KOSELLECK, Reinhart. *Past future: a contribution to the semantics of historical time.* Pontifical Catholic University of Rio de Janeiro, 2006

MARICATO, Emilia [et al]. *Rebel Cities: Passe Livre and the demonstrations that took to the streets of Brazil.* Sao Paulo: Boitempo : Carta Maior, 2013.

MEDICI, EMILIO GARRASTAZU. *The sign of Amanhd.* National Press Department, 1972

MEDICI, EMILIO GARRASTAZU. *New Consciousness of Brazil.* National Press Department, 1970.

MEDICI, EMILIO GARRASTAZU. *Tarefa de todos nos.* National Press Department, 2ª ed, 1973.

MONTEGRO, ANTONIO. *History and Memory of Political Struggles in Marcas da Memoria: Oral History of Amnesty in Brazil.* Recife: Ed. Universitaria da UFPE, 2012. MONTEGRO, Antonio. *Historia e Memoria de Lutas Politicas* in Marcas da Memoria: Historia Oral da Anistia no Brasil. Recife: Ed. Universitaria da UFPE, 2012.

MOTTA, Rodrigo Patto Sa. *As universidades e o regime militar: cultura politica brasileira e modernizagdo autoritaria.* Rio de Janeiro: Zahar, 2014

MOTTA, Rodrigo Patto Sa. *On guard against the "red danger": anti-communism in Brazil, 1917-1964.* Perspectiva Publishing House, 2002.

PRESOT, Aline Alves. *The marches of the family with God for freedom and the military coup of 1964.* Master's thesis, Postgraduate Program in History, UFRJ, Rio de Janeiro, 2004.

REIS FILHO, Daniel Aarao. *Dictatorship and democracy in Brazil: from the 1964 coup to the 1988 Constitution.* Rio de Janeiro: Zahar, 2014.

REIS FILHO, Daniel Aarao. *Military dictatorship, the left and society.* Zahar, 2000;

REZENDE, MARIA JOSE DE. *The military dictatorship in Brazil: repression and pretenses of legitimacy 1964 - 1984.* Londrina: UEL, 2001.

STUDART, Hugo. *The law of the jungle,* Sao Paulo: Geragao Editorial, 2006.

VENTURA, Zuenir. *1968 - the year that never ended.* Editora Nova Fronteira. Rio de Janeiro, 1988

I want morebooks!

Buy your books fast and straightforward online - at one of world's fastest growing online book stores! Environmentally sound due to Print-on-Demand technologies.

Buy your books online at
www.morebooks.shop

Kaufen Sie Ihre Bücher schnell und unkompliziert online – auf einer der am schnellsten wachsenden Buchhandelsplattformen weltweit! Dank Print-On-Demand umwelt- und ressourcenschonend produziert.

Bücher schneller online kaufen
www.morebooks.shop

Printed by Books on Demand GmbH, Norderstedt / Germany